Autobiography as
Indigenous
Intellectual
Tradition

Indigenous Studies Series

The Indigenous Studies Series builds on the successes of the past and is inspired by recent critical conversations about Indigenous epistemological frameworks. Recognizing the need to encourage burgeoning scholarship, the series welcomes manuscripts drawing upon Indigenous intellectual traditions and philosophies, particularly in discussions situated within the Humanities.

Series Editor

Dr. Deanna Reder (Cree-Metis), Associate Professor, First Nations Studies and English, Simon Fraser University

Advisory Board

Dr. Jo-ann Archibald (Sto:lō), Professor of Educational Studies, Faculty of Education, University of British Columbia

Dr. Kristina Bidwell (NunatuKavut), Associate Dean of Aboriginal Affairs, College of Arts and Science, Professor of English, University of Saskatchewan

Dr. Daniel Heath Justice (Cherokee Nation), Professor, First Nations and Indigenous Studies/English, Canada Research Chair in Indigenous Literature and Expressive Culture, University of British Columbia

Dr. Eldon Yellowhorn (Piikani), Associate Professor, Archaeology, Director of First Nations Studies, Simon Fraser University

Autobiography as
Indigenous
Intellectual
Tradition
Cree and Métis âcimisowina

Deanna Reder

WILFRID LAURIER
UNIVERSITY PRESS

This book has been published with the help of a grant from the Canadian Federation for the Humanities and Social Sciences, through the Awards to Scholarly Publications Program, using funds provided by the Social Sciences and Humanities Research Council of Canada. Wilfrid Laurier University Press acknowledges the support of the Canada Council for the Arts for our publishing program. We acknowledge the financial support of the Government of Canada through the Canada Book Fund for our publishing activities. Funding provided by the Government of Ontario and the Ontario Arts Council. This work was supported by the Research Support Fund.

Funded by the Government of Canada

Library and Archives Canada Cataloguing in Publication

Title: Autobiography as Indigenous intellectual tradition : Cree and Métis âcimisowina / Deanna Reder.

Names: Reder, Deanna, 1963- author.

Description: Series statement: Indigenous studies series | Includes bibliographical references and index.

Identifiers: Canadiana (print) 20210335025 | Canadiana (ebook) 20210341572 | ISBN 9781771125543 (softcover) | ISBN 9781771125550 (EPUB) | ISBN 9781771125567 (PDF)

Subjects: LCSH: Métis—Biography—History and criticism. | LCSH: Métis—Intellectual life. | LCSH: Autobiography. | LCSH: Biography as a literary form. | CSH: First Nations—Canada—Biography—History and criticism. | CSH: First Nations—Canada—Intellectual life. | CSH: Métis authors. | CSH: First Nations authors—Canada.

Classification: LCC E89.5 .R43 2022 | DDC 971.004/97—dc23

Cover design and interior design by Angela Booth Malleau. Front cover image by George Littlechild

This book is printed on FSC® certified paper. It contains recycled materials and other controlled sources, is processed chlorine-free, and is manufactured using biogas energy.

Printed in Canada

Wilfrid Laurier University Press is located on the Haldimand Tract, part of the traditional territories of the Haudenosaunee, Anishinaabe, and Neutral peoples. This land is part of the Dish with One Spoon Treaty between the Haudenosaunee and Anishnaabe peoples and symbolizes the agreement to share, to protect our resources, and not to engage in conflict. We are grateful to the Indigenous peoples who continue to care for and remain interconnected with this land. Through the work we publish in partnership with our authors, we seek to honour our local and larger community relationships, and to engage with the diversity of collective knowledge integral to responsible scholarly and cultural exchange.

Dedication

For Eric Davis, for everything

Contents

Glossary of Cree Terms[1]

âcimisowin(a)
  story (stories) about oneself/autobiography (autobiographies)
âcimowin(a)
  factual story (stories)
âniskwâcimopicikêwin
  the process or act of interconnecting stories together, similar to
  inter-textuality but not limited to text only
âpihtawikosisân(ak)
  Métis; Métis person, Métis people
âtayôhkêwin(a)
  sacred story (stories)
awîna mâka kiya?
  Who is it that you really are?
câpân(ak)
  great-grandparent(s); also, reciprocally great-grandchild(ren)
ê-kî-mâyahkâmikahk
  when it went wrong; 1885
iskwêw(ak)
  woman (women)
kakêskihkêmowin(a)
  counselling lecture(s)
kâ-pitikow
  Chief Thunderchild
kayâs-âcimowin(a)
  historical account(s)
kihcêyihtamowin
  respect between people
kiskêyihtamowin
  knowledge, experience, learning
kiwâhkômâkaninawak
  all our collective relations (plural possessive)
kiyâm
  oh well, it's okay, never mind, let it be
kwayaskwastâsowin
  the act of putting something right
mahkesîs(ak)
  fox(es)

mâhtâhitowin
   give-away
mêmêkwêsiw(ak)
   one (or more) of the sacred little people
nâpêw
   a man
nâpêwatisowin
   man ways
nêhiyaw(ak)
   Cree; Cree person (people)
nêhiyawêwin
   Cree language
nêhiyawi-itâpisinowin
   Cree worldview or way of seeing
nêhiyawi-mâmitonêyihcikan
   Cree consciousness or thinking
nêhiyâwiwin
   being Cree, Cree identity, Creeness, Indianness
niwâhkômâkan(ak)
   my relation(s)
nôcihitowi-pîsim
   the Mating Moon; September
okihcihtâw(ak)
   warrior(s), worthy young man (men)
pâhkahkos(ak)
   bony spectre(s), Hunger Spirit(s)
piyêsiw(ak)
   Thunderbird(s)
wâhkôhtowin
   interrelatedness of all things
wawiyatâcimowin(a)
   funny little stories
wêwêpison
   hammock, often made for babies
wîhtikow(ak)
   Windigo(s), cannibal spirit(s)
wîsahkêcâhk
   Elder Brother/ Sacred Being

*ispîhk awiyak ê-âcimostâsk ohcitaw piko ta-natohtawat, ta-kiskisiyan,
ta-kiskinwahamâkosiyan êkota ohci; nawac mihcêtwâw kâ-pêhtaman
âcimowin, nawac ohcitaw piko kîsta êwako ta-âcimoyan.*

*When someone shares a story with you, you have an obligation
to listen, to remember it, to learn from it;
the more often a story is repeated to you, the more obligation.*

She Told Us Stories Constantly
Autobiography as Methodology

When I was a child my mother slept a lot. It is hard for me to judge whether she slept more or less at certain times in my life, but it is generally true that I would find her napping on the couch when I came home from school. This is not to say that I found her sleeping unusual—I generally did not think about it much at all.

For most of my childhood, we lived in little houses on Canadian army bases called Private Married Quarters, or PMQs. Wherever we were stationed, we lived in neighbourhoods with homes placed snugly together, the playgrounds packed with roaming children, all with fathers who worked at the same place. All of this changed in grade five when my parents bought their first house, built on a quarter-acre lot, in the outskirts of a small city on Vancouver Island. There were apple and plum trees, woods behind us, an empty lot full of blackberry bushes on one side, and neighbours we rarely spoke to on the other. My father tilled the soil to make a gigantic garden, and we got a dog.

Because Mom didn't work outside the home and didn't drive, she had considerably fewer opportunities to see other people than when we lived on the base. She no longer had other military wives to have tea with, and my brother and I could no longer go outside and find playmates within arm's reach. At some point, I told her that she was depressed and bored and she told me that she was fine and that I was the one who was unhappy. While I remember these words, I easily dismissed them because it seemed to me that given her complete lack of autonomy—town was too far for her to walk to, she was physically unable to go anywhere unless my father or her friends drove her, her sole source of income was the grocery money my father gave her on payday—she had to have felt trapped.

I never questioned why it was that she couldn't walk into town, but this was just something Mom didn't do. She had weak ankles and couldn't go that far. Part of the reason could have been because of her weight. Pictures from her wedding show her as a slender twenty-year-old who was five feet four and one hundred pounds. By the time I was in kindergarten and she was not yet thirty, she was double that amount, a weight she fought most of her adult life. She was a member of TOPS—Take Off Pounds Sensibly—and went every Wednesday night for a weigh-in and an evening with the girls. Some weeks Mom lost a few pounds and was that week's "greatest loser," and other weeks she gained a few and would come home and sigh. That being said, I never remember Mom overeating. She seemed to have no compulsion to snack or eat sweets, but the fact that she was heavy was proof positive of her need to diet. At the age of eleven, I joined the pre-teen TOPS group and I still credit the weekly weigh-ins and the tricks I learned to fool the scale as the source of years of panic around my weight.

Because my dad had his own demons, he was only supportive intermittently. Sometimes, inspired by his military training, he would cajole her into exercising more to drop the weight. When as a pre-teen I lost thirteen pounds, he would refer to me and praise my self-discipline, suggesting that Mom take a page out of my book. "Willpower" was the buzzword. You had to have willpower.

What really changed our family's eating habits, however, was my dad's first heart attack at the age of forty-two, when I was in grade seven. After that, Mom rarely cooked with the frying pan, and she never again made corned beef and cabbage—the meat was too fatty and salty   and she started to use whole wheat flour when she baked bread. She still used white flour and lard to make bannock, though, and when Dad would go out of town, she would make pan-fried potatoes as a treat.

My parents didn't consider modern conveniences necessary. Dad liked to chop wood with an axe; in the garden, other than using a rototiller once a year, he worked the soil using a shovel and a hoe. And until his death in the mid-1980s, Mom used a wringer washing machine and, in the summer, a clothesline. She canned everything from plums and bread-and-butter pickles to apple butter and blackberry jam. While she would try the fancy Duncan Hines cake mixes and the occasional Hamburger Helper, she always made her own pastry for her pies and wouldn't think of buying a chicken that was already cut up because that was a waste of money.

Still, if Dad had been drinking, he would get into a tirade about how messy the house was and accuse Mom of laziness and lack of ambition, attributing it to the fact that she was an Indian. "They didn't even have the wheel, for Christ sakes," he would say. Sometimes she would yell back at him, but usually she would say nothing and reprimand me if I said anything. "He just wants someone to argue with," she would tell me.

Because it was difficult to explain Mom's lack of energy—there were lots of things that my friends' mothers could do that Mom didn't—the charge of laziness worried me. The fact that she was the anchor in the family, running the household, making much of our meals from scratch, while balancing out my dad's moods or my brother's tribulations at school, all the while never turning away anyone at mealtime or ever refusing anyone a cup of tea, I am ashamed to say, I never appreciated as work.

It was only when my Auntie Alice, eighteen years older than Mom, became bedridden in her fifties that we began to understand exactly how myotonic dystrophy affects a person. Most people, including our family doctor, understood Duchenne syndrome, a form of muscular dystrophy that affects children. But few knew the characteristics of myotonic dystrophy: how it only takes effect in adulthood, slowing down one's metabolism and sapping one's energy as one's muscles slowly waste away. Even fewer knew that there was a particular syndrome for sons of affected mothers. From childhood, these boys lack energy and muscle tone, which along with other health complications, hampers their progress in learning and in school. Even though in the early 1980s most branches of our family provided blood samples to determine how extensively this disease had hit us, no one could imagine that two decades later, only one of my mother's nine brothers and sisters would survive. Neither could anyone imagine just how differently the disease would affect each sibling. My Uncle Dave could use a walker to get around at age sixty but had trouble swallowing food. My Mom, like Auntie Alice, could still eat and drink but was bedridden by age fifty-eight and could not so much as adjust her head if it slipped off a pillow. And of all the aunts, uncles, and cousins, my brother is the first to have issues with his heart and lungs.

When I think about how I have described my childhood and my family in the past, I cannot help but notice how my versions of these stories have shifted over the years. As a teenager I became religious and believed that my family needed salvation and the grace of God. As a young woman, my religious devotion waned and feminism provided a more compelling critique. I began to notice how, because of my mother's role in our family, she was bereft of economic opportunities, with no access to resources that could alleviate some of our distresses. I became more critical of patriarchy and the military-industrial complex that during the Cold War sent my father, a teenager at the time with a grade six education, into battle, in an army culture that encouraged drinking to deal with the emotional fallout.

If I ever thought to frame our family story as an illness narrative, I would have, in earlier years, focused on heart disease, alcoholism, or perhaps learning disabilities or eating disorders. Until I was in my twenties, I couldn't have discussed the effects of myotonic dystrophy because we didn't know what they were. While I now recognize how this disease affected us, I am hard pressed to dismiss previous versions, previous interpretations. Other illnesses did impact our family. And it wasn't wrong, I think, to hope for divine intervention or acknowledge the oppressive forces that bore down upon us. But just as I truly appreciate how devastating myotonic dystrophy has been to our family, I also recognize that far more influential on our lives than this disease, and subsequently Mom's weakness, were her strengths. Along with her ability to bear hardship was her talent at storytelling. Mom told us stories constantly, over dinner, over cups of tea, over games of Rummy or Trouble. Because of the many forces that conspired to keep her at home, she was usually there, and she would constantly talk about her life, focusing especially on her childhood, our family, our aunts and uncles and grandparents and other relations. In contrast, Dad didn't talk much about his childhood, but Mom shared what she learned from her visits with his side of the family. We all—Dad included—loved to hear her tell her stories because she was so funny.

What I recognize now is that even though she rarely spoke Cree unless her siblings were around, she drew on Cree storytelling traditions to entertain and share with us, as a way to encourage and be with us. Of the generic categories described by linguist H. C. Wolfart,[1] she never told âtayôhkêwina,[2] Cree sacred stories that often feature the trickster, wîsahkêcâhk. In fact, she insisted that wîsahkêcâhk was just like Santa Claus and nothing to worry about. Neither did she tell us kayâs-âcimowina, historical accounts, or kakêskihkêmowina, which is counsel. Rarely would Mom dispense advice, and while her stories revealed her understanding of what was good or bad, she never told morality tales: she was always hesitant to tell other people what to do. When as a little girl I asked her who I should marry when I grew up, her response was typical of her: "It doesn't matter to me," she said. "I don't have to live with him."

Instead, what Mom told were âcimowina, which are stories or accounts of daily life, although "in this genre the supernatural is decidedly a part of the factual world."[3] Mom relied heavily on âcimisowina, especially a sub-genre of autobiographical storytelling that was humorous. Wolfart explains:

> Autobiographical texts commonly take the form either of wawi-yatâcimowin, 'funny story' or an âcimisowin, a 'story about oneself,' told in self-mocking detachment, which lets the audience laugh along with the narrator about some misfortune he or she suffered.[4]

Sometimes Mom's stories would sound rude if you didn't understand the context. There was the time when one of my aunties went to the outhouse in the middle of the night, only to sit down on a family friend who had fallen asleep. Or there was the time one of my cousins decided to use bug spray to cure a sexually transmitted disease, only to find it burned his groin so badly that he had to run all the way from my grandparent's house down to the lake to wash it off. It is hard to tell stories like Mom did. What she retold might be embarrassing, but it was never mocking; it might be teasing, but it was never attacking or mean-spirited; all of it, including stories of her own escapades and misadventures, were part of the shared hilarity of life. She told family stories from her perspective as the youngest of ten, with a strong, powerful mother and a quiet, gentle father, growing up around the drama of her nine older siblings and then an increasing cluster of young nieces and nephews. As in any storytelling tradition, meaning was added by her inflection, the rolling of her eyes, the way she would exhale to dismiss something that was ridiculous. Amazingly, she rarely told the same story in exactly the same way, but each time emphasized and re-emphasized different points.

Métis philosopher Lorraine Brundige (now Mayer) emphasizes the profound lessons embedded in stories, including âcimowina (factual stories), âcimisowina (personal, autobiographical stories), and wawiyatâcimowina (funny, humorous personal stories); she writes that:

> Although âcimowin[a], even wawiyatâcimisowin[a] were often told by specialists, the historians and teachers, our families and others in our communities were also regarded as teachers. And, though these stories were more often of a personal nature, nonetheless they were/are equally filled with metaphysical, epistemological and ethical lessons.[5]

While never overtly didactic, I have come to realize how much I learned about the world, my family, and my place in both through Mom's tutelage. On those times when I would be reunited with family, I could recognize at least some of the underlying assumptions embedded in nêhiyaw thinking; from family storytelling I learned about the need to listen; I was cautious about asking too often for explanations because much of the work of interpretation was my responsibility. Besides, it can be hard to nail down meanings that by nature can shift and change.

Partly because I was raised listening to my mother's âcimisowin, I was not surprised that many of the Indigenous authors in Canada I had begun reading as an adult included—and relied upon—their own life stories. Whatever the genre—be it history, political commentary, public address, literary criticism, or journalism—I noted that writing by Indigenous authors integrated autobiographical detail. I always recognized both the self-worth and high regard for the opinions of others implicit in this practice. What did surprise me, however, was that this archive has been understudied and undervalued.

Identifying this neglect as a gap in the scholarship and therefore an ideal research topic, I decided to complete graduate work on autobiographies by Indigenous authors. In my original conceptualization of this project, I noted that while several studies of Native American autobiographies had been completed since the 1970s, no similar work existed in Canada. I presumed, at the time, that I could build on American scholarship and analyze differences between autobiographies by Native Americans in the United States and those by Indigenous authors north of the border. I planned to draw on the techniques developed by autobiography theorists to measure their effectiveness and relevance to the concerns of Indigenous works.

Instead, I found that Native American autobiography studies and autobiography theory have been severely limited by the lack of Indigenous perspectives. I acknowledge a debt to feminist standpoint theory that helped me articulate this problem and modelled a version of criticism that included references to autobiography as a way to subvert the convention of writing from a distance, in an apparently detached or neutral way.[6]

As Sharon Crasnow summarizes:

> Feminist standpoint methodology not only directs researchers to start from the lives of women but also to produce knowledge for, by, and about women. Spelling out in what way knowledge might be for, by, and about women is part of what goes into building a bridge from methodology (how to do research) to epistemology (how and why doing research in this way produces knowledge). Knowledge that starts from the lives of women and produces knowledge for women is socially situated. Thus feminist standpoint approaches appear to involve two theses: (1) a situated knowledge thesis and (2) a thesis of epistemic advantage.[7]

In particular I was encouraged by Donna Haraway's idea of situated knowledge that posited that those who are oppressed—those who speak from the "vantage point of the subjugated"—are better able to critique power structures.[8] The idea that feminist scholars could argue and advocate for the participation of women as researchers and theorists inspired me to argue and advocate for the prioritization of Indigenous perspectives.

The insights of standpoint theory emboldened me to use my *âcimisowin* as a method of reorienting academic inquiry. Instead of considering my experiences as a deficiency, I began to consider my life story as method, as a tool to rely upon when evaluating texts by Indigenous writers. Métis scholar Warren Cariou provides a caution in his 2020 essay about Indigenous literary critical approaches, titled "On Critical Humility":

Though the writing (of Indigenous criticism) may take up more personal autobiographical forms in order to account for the critic's place in the relationship with the story, *it will not end up being primarily about the critic.* So much postcolonial criticism has fallen into that trap.[9]

This is because, according to Cariou, "Being a good listener is predicated upon being humble, and listening is the primary mode through which we learn the teachings that give our lives direction and meaning."[10] Cariou's insights align with the values that I learned through my mother's storytelling practice, that emphasized the value of listening and epistemic humility. Including one's story is not a way to take centre stage as much as to share and visit together. This allowed me to recognize how Indigenous authors use their life stories to question both the concept of epistemological objectivity and the tenets of white supremacy. It allowed me to value the position from which I speak, as a nêhiyaw-âpihtawikosisâniskwêw, a Cree-Métis woman who shares nêhiyawi-itâpisinowin.[11]

Once I began to value âcimisowina, I began to understand a pre-existing compulsion of mine to search out writing that reflected my family and community. I had always noticed that even though the Cree language, nêhiyawêwin, was predominant in my mother's generation, it was almost completely absent in the rest of the world. I noticed that the place and the people I knew in Northern Saskatchewan, who featured large in my mother's stories, were seemingly unknown in references I consulted or in lessons at school. This was momentarily resolved when I heard Cree spoken on TV—once while watching a Hollywood western, a Cree-speaker, cast as an Indian Chief, actually spoke nêhiyawêwin, and Mom was able to translate for us. This desire of mine to collect any book that referenced Cree or Métis people or places was a way to collect evidence that this world I knew exists.

By the 1990s, just as Indigenous literatures began to be increasingly taught in university courses, Indigenous scholars proposed that different literary approaches would need to be developed than those honed for studying William Shakespeare, Jane Austen, or Margaret Atwood. Indigenous theorists proposed that worldviews from specific tribal traditions could be used to study or decode works by authors of that nation—an approach called Indigenous literary nationalism.[12] It was a strategy that asked readers to think of the multiple cultures that exist on Turtle Island, rather than understand "Indigenous literature" as a monolithic category. Indigenous literary nationalism encouraged literary scholars to look beyond evidence of the common experience of colonization in our writing and instead to think about specific expressions of nation or tribal-specific worldviews.

It was at this point that drawing on my own experience, my âcimisowin, became a benefit, allowing me to identify intellectual traditions that share nêhiyawi-itâpisinowin. In my family's experience, many of my generation and younger do not speak much Cree anymore, and many have never had the chance to learn Cree story cycles. When I examined this writing, I knew that I could not rely on the presence of the Cree language and stories from the Cree canon, as sole markers of the influence of Cree ideas, given the complicated history of linguicide, foundational to colonizing efforts by the Church and State.

Expressions of the value of the Cree language and language preservation in Cree and Cree-Métis writing do exist. In the preface to an anthology of Indigenous women's writing published in 1990, titled "Here are our Voices— Who Will Hear?", Métis scholar and poet Emma LaRocque declared:

> My first language is Plains Cree. My parents were forced to allow me to go to school where I was forced to learn English. In that time, I have "appropriated" this language without abandoning my Cree. I have sought to master this language.[13]

Still, even though LaRocque has mastered both Cree and English, and has spent her career teaching Indigenous literatures at the University of Manitoba, her teaching and most of her poetry and scholarship are written in English, likely because she is addressing readers who do not have her fluency.

And the value of the Cree canon is expressed in some nêhiyaw writing. Tomson Highway, for example, uses the Cree language and retells trickster stories throughout his novel, *Kiss of the Fur Queen* (1998). Louise Halfe relies on Cree to retell Rolling Head stories in her poems in *The Crooked Good* (2007). Yet many nêhiyawak do not know Cree sacred stories because, as LaRocque explains,

> Literature is political in that its linguistic and ideological transmission is defined and determined by those in power. This is why Shakespeare rather than Wisakehcha [the Cree trickster][14] is classified as 'classical' in our school curriculum.[15]

This, by the way, is not simply true in residential schools of the past. It is rare to find, in present-day public schools and universities, instructors with expertise to teach stories about wîsahkêcâhk as part of classic Cree story cycles.

In my search to identify common attributes of Cree and Métis writing, I knew through family experience not to expect that the Cree language and Cree sacred stories would be necessary features. Instead, what I typically could expect to find in Cree and Métis writing, as foundational to shared intellectual traditions, is âcimisowina, or life stories. For example, LaRocque's preface includes reference to her experiences; the story arc of Highway's novel is a fictionalized version of his life story; and Halfe identifies the influence of the Creation Legend on her identity as a Cree woman in her keynote address on Rolling Head.[16]

Likewise, in the body of Cree writing collected by Cree linguist Freda Ahenakew, âcimisowina are prominent. Beginning in 1987, she helped release almost a dozen works over the next twenty years, published bilingually in both English and Cree, several of which are life stories: *Our Grandmothers' Lives, as Told in Their Own Words* (1992); *The Cree Language is our Identity: the La Ronge Lectures of Sarah Whitecalf* (1993); *Their Example Showed Me the Way: A Cree Woman's Life Shaped by Two Cultures* (1997) by Emma Minde; *They Knew Both Sides of Medicine: Cree Tales of Curing and Cursing Told by Alice Ahenakew* (2000). In their comments on Minde's life story, Ahenakew and co-editor H.C. Wolfart describe *Their Example Showed Me the Way* as "classical in form; within the overall genre of âcimowin ... she alternates between the autobiographical text or âcimisowin and the counselling text or kakêskihkêmowin."[17] In Freda Ahenakew's significant body of work, the inclusion of âcimisowin is even more popular than the telling of sacred Cree stories, possibly because of the protocols that surround telling âtayôhkêwina.

From this introductory glance at the work of Cree and Métis authors like Campbell, LaRocque, Highway, Halfe, and Freda Ahenakew, I conclude that âcimisowin *is a* preferred genre. One of my objectives in this book is to examine previously known work—like that by Maria Campbell and Harold Cardinal—in a new light, alongside hitherto neglected or completely unknown work that has never been published—such as writing by James Settee, Edward Ahenakew, and James Brady—to explore the influence of Cree concepts in their autobiographical writing.

Among other purposes, this book is meant to be a contribution to Indigenous cultural resurgence that emphasizes the value of Indigenous knowledges, which are inseparable from Indigenous languages. Envisioned as a support for language revitalization, each chapter is grounded by a concept expressed in nêhiyawêwin. I do this in full recognition that I remain an introductory language learner and must rely on those who are more proficient in the language than I might ever be.

As I discuss the following authors, I have decided not to separate Settee, Ahenakew, and Cardinal (and Absolom Halkett) on one side as Cree, and Campbell and Brady on the other as Métis, given that they all draw on similar

worldviews—ways of knowing or ways of seeing (nêhiyawi-itâpisinowin)—
that emerge from a common language spoken in similar parts of the world.
Instead, I wonder how we might think of these authors as intellectuals whose
ideas are drawn from and inspired by a common worldview and a common
language: nêhiyawêwin.

It might seem on the face of it that I am working against Métis scholars and leaders who are defining themselves as different from First Nations
in general (and Cree or Anishinaabe in particular). However, it is because
I recognize the need for Indigenous political aspirations to be located in
Indigenous concepts that I offer this study. I think of the June 2021 address
by Maria Campbell to the members of the Federation for the Humanities
and Social Sciences, as part of their annual "Big Thinking" lectures, titled
"Ni'wahkomakanak: All My Relations."[18] Campbell began by stating that
niwâhkômâkanak,

> [meaning "all my relations"] included territories with rivers, creeks,
> lakes, hills, rocks, plants, and all the creatures on it. We understood
> and lived that word, celebrating with visiting, feasting, and helping
> each other, regardless of differences. Our old people reminding us
> family was the most important thing. I was twelve years old when
> that started to change in our area, beginning with the state scooping
> of children and forcing our people off the land and families migrat-
> ing to urban centres to find work. Boundaries made of policies and
> laws divided us and worst of all, we started to believe that these
> divisions defined us.... This presentation is about my family and
> how we became us and them.

The labels of status, non-status, and Métis each serve to alienate us from each
other and from our land and all our relations.[19] The following examination
rejects the divisions caused by differing state-imposed legal identities on
members of the same family and community. I rely on the predominance of
the Cree language and concepts in my Cree-speaking Cree and Métis family,
and by extension in the writing of the authors I discuss, as a contribution to
strengthening Indigenous intellectual and political sovereignty.

As for Métis fights for self-determination, specifically, I have been privileged to hear about several struggles and successes over decades. To begin
with, my Uncle Frank's father was Peter Tomkins,[20] one of the Famous Five
Métis activists who made political gains in Alberta in the 1930s. Frank grew
up during this time period and as an adult remained close with his father's
fellow activists, Malcolm Norris and Jim Brady.[21] He also told me about how,
on April 9, 1981,[22] he went as provincial secretary of the Métis delegation,
along with the president of the Association of Métis and Non-Status Indians

Fig. 1 The Métis delegation in London, England in 1981. Left to right: Frank Tomkins, provincial secretary and meeting organizer; Rod Bishop, board member; Jim Sinclair, president of the Métis and Non-Status Indians of Saskatchewan; Jim Durocher, treasurer, and Wayne McKenzie, board member. Reprinted with permission of the Gabriel Dumont Institute.

of Saskatchewan (AMNSIS), Jim Sinclair, treasurer Jim Durocher, and board members Rod Bishop and Wayne McKenzie, to meet with the House of Lords All Party Committee charged with the patriation of the Constitution of Canada. Together they plead their case, arguing that rights for Métis and Non-Status people ought to be enshrined in Canada's 1982 constitution. In his article about the 1981 meeting, Skip Hambling, communications advisor for the delegation, confirms their success. He writes in *The New Breed* that:

> In all their months of lobbying in England, no Indian or Native Peoples group has done better—some not as well—and AMNSIS has managed it all in three days. The presentation by AMNSIS on behalf of the 85,000 Metis and Non-Status Indians of Saskatchewan is, by itself a historical first. Up to now, none of the British MPs understood the difference separating the Native Council of Canada (NCC) and AMNSIS.[23]

As a gesture of high regard, the three members of the group, Uncle Frank included, took off their Métis sashes and gifted them to the British chairs of the committee.[24]

It is through his stories that I learned that Frank understood the responsibility to be a good leader for Métis people, especially at such a pivotal time. And for Frank, his family, as well as for family members from my mother's generation, Cree was their mothertongue. While some Métis communities spoke Michif, my family was more closely allied to the Cree language— nêhiyawêwin. In fact, it was Uncle Frank's assertion that the Métis protected nêhiyawêwin at a time when Status people could not. Frank explained that growing up he spoke Cree in day-to-day discussions at home and was never overtly coerced to abandon his language. This is in contrast to Status Indians under the Indian Act, who were forced to attend residential school where English was the lingua franca, and speaking of Indigenous languages was suppressed. Métis fluency in Cree is why, according to Frank, the United States army recruited his older brother Charles (also called Checker), along with several young Métis men, to serve as Cree code-talkers during the Second World War.[25] Because Checker was fluent, he and other Cree code-talkers were able to pass secret messages quickly over the airwaves to each other on behalf of the Allies without being understood by German troops.[26]

This point does not negate the fact that there exist Métis communities who speak Michif or Anishinaabemowin or another Indigenous language. It simply was not the experience of our family.[27] During my mother's generation, our family spoke Cree, as well as English. If I wished to identify factions within our family, it wouldn't be between those who identify as Cree and those who identify as Métis. Instead, there is a generational and linguistic divide between those in my mother's generation—Cree and Métis— who were fluent in nêhiyawêwin and would identify nêhiyawêwin as their mother tongue, as compared with those in my and my cousins' generation who generally do not speak the language. But there are signs of language revitalization, as demonstrated in the recent increase of people who use the Cree word for Cree, which is "nêhiyaw" and the Cree word for Métis, which is "âpihtawikosisân." If nêhiyawêwin is to be retained in our family, regardless of how we identify, it will have to be work taken up by the next generation—our children and grandchildren.

Rather than focus on the ways that separate us, I think about the Cree and Métis writers I discuss as related, all who see the world through a Cree worldview, through nêhiyawi-itâpisinowin. Prioritizing the Cree language, nêhiyawêwin, I structure the work of each of the following chapters around a Cree concept. Implicit in this is the prioritization of Cree intellectual and cultural perspectives that considers one's identity and position to be a central rather than peripheral concern in research.

Chapter One, "âcimisowin as Indigenous Intellectual Tradition: From George Copway to James Settee," situates specifically Cree and Cree-Métis lifewriting in a broader Indigenous context. I begin with a discussion of the first book by an Indigenous author published in lands now claimed by Canada—Anishinaabe writer George Copway's autobiography, first published in 1847—offering a thematic comparison with a previously unstudied autobiographical essay by Cree writer James Settee, circa 1890. I emphasize the need to prioritize Indigenous perspectives of the historical context when we read Indigenous autobiographies, rather than adopt narratives that support colonial perspectives. For example, while the influence of the Church is often considered a central concern in the writing of Copway and Settee, both Protestant ministers, the effects upon their communities of land theft and the collapse of Indigenous economic systems are not often appreciated as equally relevant. Copway and Settee did not abandon Indigenous worldviews in favour of Christianized, Western epistemologies. Instead, living at a time of catastrophe, they relied on cultural teachings to imagine a way through the chaos.[28] Both reject alcohol, which was creating frightening social environments, and enthusiastically learn to read and write in English. I then include a discussion of the embrace of Cree syllabics, something that has been understood by nêhiyawak as writing that pre-existed contact, so that the acts of reading and writing, in whatever language and by whatever technology, are by extension Cree acts.

Chapter Two examines the function of wâhkôhtowin in Maria Campbell's *Halfbreed*, the most famous Indigenous autobiography in Canada. I draw on the discussion of wâhkôhtowin in the work of Métis and Cree scholars like Brenda Macdougall, Neal McLeod, and Tasha Beeds to contextualize Campbell's understanding of the interrelatedness of all things. I also draw on the work of Métis philosopher Lorraine Brundige, who identifies the understanding of multiple perspectives as a foundational aspect of Cree theory. I think about Campbell's tactics of social protest and defiance, contextualized by her long-standing complaint that a passage from *Halfbreed*, incriminating the RCMP, had been expurgated against her wishes in 1973.[29] Although her publishing house had insisted that any copy of the passage that Campbell had written about sexual violence had been destroyed, my then research assistant, Alix Shield, was able to locate the excised passage and, following Indigenous protocols, return it to Campbell, which initiated the publication of a new edition of *Halfbreed* in 2019. In the recounting of genealogies, Campbell demonstrates the multiple obligations of wâhkôhtowin, of interrelatedness; the story about the removal without consent of Campbell's account of her sexual assault in the 1973 edition demonstrates the ways in which her publishing house ignored its obligations to her.

Chapter Three is titled "Respectful Interaction and Tolerance for Different Perspectives: kihcêyihtamowin in Edward Ahenakew's *Old Keyam*." I examine Ahenakew's work, and in particular his unpublished, handwritten manuscript about a character named Old Keyam, who effectively acts as his author's mouthpiece, sharing opinions that Ahenakew, as an Anglican cleric and Status Indian, would not be at liberty to articulate. This autobiographical fiction was originally intended to stand on its own and to be published in the 1920s, but it did not find publication until it was edited by Ruth M. Buck after Ahenakew's death as the second half of *Voices of the Plains Cree* (1973). I suggest that the confusing and sometimes contradictory shifts of opinion in the text exist for two reasons: first, some can be considered in light of Cree values, in which Ahenakew prioritizes respectful interactions through the toleration of different points of view; second, editor Ruth M. Buck introduced contradictions through her edits, resulting in more judgmental statements than what Ahenakew would have endorsed. I compare the original and the published, edited version to unveil Ahenakew's perspective. I also use the cultural value of kihcêyihtamowin, respect between people, to understand the character of Old Keyam, not as defeated but rather strengthened by his commitment to his Cree identity. By doing so, I wish to celebrate Edward Ahenakew as a leading Cree intellectual, whose own ambitions as a writer were foiled by the publishing industry.

Chapter Four, "Edward Ahenakew's Intertwined Unpublished Life-Inspired Stories: âniskwâcimopicikêwin in *Black Hawk* and *Old Keyam*," I consider two largely unpublished works by the under-published author, that are so interrelated through intertextual allusions that the only way to understand one is to read the other, like Cree story cycles where settings and episodes in one story are revisited or continued in the other. This is a significant first attempt to understand the Ahenakew corpus and to do so from a nêhiyaw perspective. The first story, *Black Hawk*, is an unpublished semi-autobiographical novel written circa 1914 to 1918.[30] I compare this text with the *Old Keyam* manuscript,[31] written in the 1920s and never published in full, rather than rely on the section titled "Old Keyam," published as the second half of *Voices of the Plains Cree*, which was heavily edited by Buck and released in 1973, twelve years after Ahenakew's passing; my discussion evaluates three manuscript chapters of *Old Keyam* that Buck intentionally omitted. Through my comparison of Ahenakew's two unpublished manuscripts, I am able to identify the interconnections and intertextuality—how âniskwâcimopicikêwin functions—that Ahenakew envisioned, a vision that has been undermined by a neglectful publishing industry and destructive editing practices.

Chapter Five, "How âcimisowin Preserves History: James Brady, Papaschase, and Absolom Halkett," looks at the variety of autobiographical acts completed by Brady, an effective Métis political activist, a Communist, as well as a noted bibliophile, researcher, writer, and intellectual. Although he was uniquely positioned to write about his own life and that of a family friend, Chief Papaschase, whom he refers to as Papasschayo, in the context of the settlement of Western Canada, Brady consistently had trouble being published. But at least his writing has been preserved in the archive. In comparison, very little is recorded about his friend and Cree business partner, Absolom Halkett, who went prospecting with Brady in 1967 at Lower Foster Lake in Northern Saskatchewan, only for the two of them to disappear without a trace.[32] This chapter considers the ways in which âcimisowina document stories about people and events that otherwise would be forgotten.

In Chapter Six, "kiskêyihtamowin: Seekers of Knowledge, Cree Intergenerational Inquiry, Shared by Harold Cardinal," I consider what it means to be nêhiyaw.[33] I contrast renowned lawyer Harold Cardinal's discussion of the Cree search for knowledge with my family's experiences with education, demonstrating the richness of nêhiyaw understanding of knowledge transmission as compared to the deficiencies of the public school system. Cardinal recounts an encounter between a younger version of himself and an Elder who asks him, "awîna mâka kiya?" (Who is it that you really are?).[34]

It is tempting, given Cardinal's profile and accomplishments, to identify him as an exceptional intellectual and leader. But this is not how Cardinal represents himself in his story. Instead, he is the learner, listening to his Elder and trying to understand. Cardinal's words, part reflection, part philosophy, model the intergenerational nature of kiskêyihtamowin, and reinforce the Cree worldview, nêhiyawi-itâpisinowin. His story emphasizes that nêhiyaw learners are obliged to continue prior generations' search for knowledge of the Four Worlds. I am likewise implicated in this intergenerational search.

In the following chapters, I have tried to retell some of my family's stories faithfully, along with those I tell about myself, acknowledging that like all autobiographers I can only tell this story from my point of view. This position is not static, but constantly shifting, because the world and our relationships shift and change, our bodies grow and age. In Cree understandings of identity, the capacity to change in response to the constantly changing environment is valued.[35] As we live in this state of flux, the "same" stories may mean different things to us. As we learn some things, we can also forget others.

There are several concurrent arguments in this book, each of which is interconnected. First, autobiography is a preferred genre by speakers of nêhiyawêwin. Second, speaking from one's position best captures the privileged perspective from which no one else is able to speak. Third, autobiographies—âcimisowina—best allow us to assert control over our identities, histories, and knowledge systems. It is an act of autonomy in that it expresses the values of one's own story while at the same time an act of generosity, of sharing, that contributes to the history of the community, often in the face of colonial narratives determined to either erase or undermine nêhiyaw presence. Fourth, Cree and Métis people, like all Indigenous peoples, embrace multiple forms of storytelling all along the oral-literary spectrum to share our perspectives and articulate nêhiyaw concepts, sometimes addressed to dominant society, sometimes to ourselves, including those in the present but also those who have left us or will come—our ancestors and descendants. Fifth, the lack of recognition of Indigenous peoples' autobiographical traditions is an erasure that makes illegible the contributions that we have made. Sixth, this lack of recognition and neglect feeds further lack of recognition of and lack of scholarly attention to existing, albeit neglected, Indigenous writing. Seventh, the lack of Indigenous perspectives in the academy contributes to erroneous assumptions about Indigenous literary production.

Some of the suppositions about Indigenous people affirm other incorrect assumptions about Indigenous literary production. The logic that Indigenous people do not write about themselves is linked to the idea that Indigenous people have not written or have not written much because "they" prefer to tell stories orally. Therefore, there is no need to conduct an archival search for historic Indigenous writing because, as an oral culture, not much was ever written in the first place. This logic then blunts any criticism of publishing infrastructure that has suppressed Indigenous writing; historically, those texts that are published are often altered through editorial and publication practices, to a standard that often interferes with the writer's intent, often softening critique of the colonizer or obscuring underlying Indigenous perspectives and epistemologies.

In the authors discussed in this study, I examine the role of the publishing industry in their work to determine how publishing has affected what is available to the public, if their work is available at all. I examine the ways in which this work expresses nation or tribal-specific concepts, privileging their perspectives. I position myself as a nêhiyaw-âpihtawikosisân scholar, not at arm's length but rather emotionally implicated, with something to contribute to these areas of study. This notion of nêhiyawi-itâpisinowin—seeing the world through a Cree worldview—best demonstrates the wâhkôhtowin (interrelatedness) of my family and âniskwâcimopicikêwin (intertextuality) in my family stories. By listening to the following âcimisowina (autobiographies), with nêhiyawi-itâpisinowin (Cree worldview), we will better understand kihcêyihtamowin (respect between people), kiskêyihtamowin (knowledge), and nêhiyawimâmitonêyihcikan, translated as nêhiyaw thinking or Cree consciousness.

ohcitaw piko ta-pakitinamahk kahkiyaw kîkwaya kâ-kî-itêyihtamahk ôhi kîkwaya ohci êkosi ta-miyo-natohtamahk âcimowin.

We have the obligation to set aside previous assumptions and concentrate on the teachings in the story.

CHAPTER ONE

âcimisowin
Autobiography as Indigenous Intellectual Tradition[1]

I grew up around my mother's stories of our family. She was the one who connected us to her nine brothers and sisters, remembering their birthdates, the names of their spouses and children, even knowing their phone numbers off by heart. And while my father talked very little about his childhood, Mom was the one who shared what she knew from her conversations with his seven brothers and sisters, with the same perfect recall. She could talk about hijinks and hard times, about things she heard and things she saw, sometimes to highlight a serious concern or a puzzling event, but often to simply share a funny story. And typically, a common theme in all the stories that involved my grandmother, or kôhkom, as we called her, was how formidable she was. Mom might talk about my grandfather with affection, but it was to share how mild-mannered and easy-going he was, non-judgemental, quiet, and kind. The real force in the family was kôhkom, who trained her eldest daughters to run the house—a necessary pooling of labour given kôhkom didn't have conveniences like running water—while she ran a trapline, delivered babies for women in the community, and made medicines.

While I remember many stories about kôhkom's work with medicines, the one that stands out is the story of how she cured a man of blindness. A young Cree man named Absolom Halkett planned to leave the north to go study, to become an Anglican minister, but his ambitions were stalled when he discovered that he was going blind. Young Absolom sought kôhkom out, hoping she could help him. I know from family photographs that Absolom knew my Uncle George and family friend Joe Bell, because we have a photo of him standing with them and my older cousins in front of a pitched tent.

When kôhkom was approached by Absolom, she wasn't sure what to do right away. She told him to give her some time to think about it. That night, kôhkom had a dream that a bear was encircled and trapped in the boughs of willows, the leaves of the willow choking him. She woke up and went and collected these leaves and made a poultice. When the young man returned, she gave him instructions to put this paste on his eyes at night and go to the

Fig. 2 Front, from left to right: Patsy Patterson, David Clinton, Richard Bell. Back: Joe Bell with Kathy Bell, Absolom Halkett, George Patterson, c. 1955. Reprinted with permission of the Patterson family.

lake every morning and wash it off. Three times he would have to do this. If it didn't work, there was nothing more she could do for him.

What always struck me was the ending. There were none of the poignant words of wisdom or satisfying emotional conclusions that I had learned to expect from a 1970s childhood of watching television. The ending was always the same, with the same anti-climactic comments: "It worked. But he never did become a minister." There wasn't a sense that this was a failure or a disappointment to anyone. So what if he didn't become a minister! What you could depend on was that it worked, that kôhkom had fixed him. Much later, I learned that the bear in Cree culture is a medicine spirit, but no one from my family ever told me this, and no one felt that this was the point of the story. The bear was what kôhkom dreamed, and "Deanna, why do you have to analyze everything?" My tendency to ask constantly for explanations was seen as intrusive, attempting to nail down meanings that by nature could shift and change. It was always clear to me that while my own act of interpretation was my responsibility, these stories didn't follow the same rules as those followed by the movies I watched or the books I would read in university.

Some of what I learned as a listener of these stories still guides me today. I learned that an important part of listening is to set aside previous assumptions about what I think is possible, imaginable, or relevant. What matters is that I listen to the teachings in the story instead of the truth value. This, by the way, does not mean that I don't believe kôhkom healed Absolom Halkett, because I do. I just don't think that it is important that others understand the story in the same way that I do. What is especially important to me is that I learned that kôhkom was strong and powerful and talented. Even so, she had to have enough humility in her work to seek direction.

Given that I grew up on or near army bases across Western Canada throughout the 1970s and early 80s, I didn't hear many other stories about Indigenous people in the public-school curriculum that I studied or in the books that I found in public libraries. The one exception was Mohawk poet E. Pauline Johnson. Like most Canadian children of my generation, I read Johnson's "The Song My Paddle Sings"[2] in elementary school. Unaware that she was also an internationally popular performer who made her final home in Vancouver, I imagined her as an Indian maiden in her canoe, paddling near my relatives on Lac La Ronge. I liked to pretend that I was an Indian princess too, and called myself Sonsary, after a heroine in a Cowboys and Indians movie; Tracey, my best friend at the time, was renamed White Dove because she was fair. My mother would make us bannock, and Tracey and I would eat it in the tent in our backyard on the army base where our fathers were stationed. We weren't the only ones "playing Indian."[3] I remember that when our family would go camping at Elk Lake outside of Edmonton, the sign pointing to the outhouses would offer the choice for either Braves or Squaws, with accompanying pictures.

The only other Indigenous author that I remember stood out in my mind because even though my mother rarely read for pleasure, there was one exception, a book she read from cover to cover as soon as she received it. Maria Campbell's *Halfbreed*, which had been released in 1973, was sent to her by one of my aunties, and Mom searched through it for the many names of friends and people she knew.

Partly because of my mother's enthusiasm when seeing some reflection of our family in Campbell's book, I had a hunch about the importance of Indigenous autobiography to Indigenous readers. In university in the 1980s, I found one of the few anthologies of Indigenous writing available: Penny Petrone's first of three path-breaking studies of Indigenous writing, *First People, First Voices*.[4] In this collection, autobiography was clearly a preferred genre for Indigenous authors. I noted recorded speeches,[5] written appeals, battle songs, letters, poems, all of which were autobiographical, as well as portions from conventional autobiographies.[6]

What stood out as remarkable was her discussion of the archive of auto-biographical works by Christianized Ojibways,[7] whom Petrone calls "the first literary coterie of Indians in Canada, and the first to write extensively in

English."[8] Anthologized here is the 1831 letter by Peter Jones about his travels in England, the Christian testimony of John Sunday circa 1837, a portion of George Henry's 1848 pamphlet about his tour in Europe, and selections of Peter Jacobs's 1852 account of his visit to Niagara Falls. It also includes selections from the first published text by a First Nations author born in what is now called Canada, George Copway's 1847 autobiography, *The Life, History, and Travels of Kah-ge-ga-gah-bowh*.[9] Also a Christian conversion narrative, it is an autobiography of emotional crisis and salvation through literacy.

Although many authors relied on their life stories, whether requesting recognition of rights or professing Christian faith, these autobiographies are often unrecognized as legitimate Indigenous genres. Influenced by scholarship on Native American autobiography in the United States, Canadian scholars have generally diminished the significance of Indigenous autobiography by defining it as derivative of European models. For example, in *Native Literature in Canada*, Penny Petrone discusses this literary flowering by Anishinaabe, or "Ojibway" writers:

> Autobiography was also a popular literary form. Because of the great interest in Indians at the time, personal histories were in demand, and autobiography achieved great popularity. It was a new form, alien to an oral heritage where the communal and collective were celebrated.[10]

Petrone does not question this point, that autobiography is alien to oral heritage. Instead, she cites the introduction to an anthology of autobiographical essays by contemporary Native authors, *I Tell You Now*, edited by Arnold Krupat and Brian Swann:[11]

> Although the tribes, like people the world over, kept material as well as mental records of collective and personal experience, the notion of telling the whole of any one individual's life or taking merely personal experience as of particular significance was, in the most literal way, foreign to them, if not also repugnant.[12]

It is worth noting that while there are numerous scholars who were foundational to the field of Native American autobiography—recognizable names include Lynne Woods O'Brien (1973), David Brumble III, Gretchen Bataille and Kathleen Sands (1984), and Hertha Dawn Wong (1992)—the most eminent scholar is Krupat, whose 1985 monograph, *For Those Who Come After: A Study of Native American Autobiography* is considered a classic.[13] It was Krupat who first articulated the idea that because "autobiography ... is a

European invention," Indian autobiographies—and here Krupat distinguishes them as collaboratively written as-told-to work as distinct from "autobiographies by [literate] Indians"[14]—are the product of "Euroamerican pressure," with "no precontact equivalents."[15] According to Krupat, all forms of autobiography are alien to contemporary Indigenous writing, as it is "marked by egocentric individualism, historicism and writing ... [none of which] has ever characterized the native cultures of the present-day United States."[16] From Krupat's perspective, writing is foreign even after the introduction of writing systems developed for Indigenous languages; for Krupat, "after Sequoyah ... devised a Cherokee syllabary ... the presence of the grapheme still signified for the Indian the cultural other, the track of the Indo-European snake in the American garden."[17] To write autobiography is to succumb to Euroamerican pressure because, as Krupat argues, writing is foreign to Native Americans and, according to Petrone as stated above, autobiography is a form "alien to an oral heritage."[18] Petrone speculates about the popularity of the genre and the strength of the market for such subject matter. However, she does not theorize how it could be that the Ojibway writers she examines, including Copway, could so quickly switch from "repugnance" of the autobiographical, as suggested by Krupat and Swann, to embrace literacy and adopt the genre of autobiography.[19] Nor does she comment on Copway's strong autobiographical impulse.

Copway writes about his yearning for an immortality that encompasses not just the Christian concept of heaven but also the ability for his words to live on after his hand "that wrote these recollections shall have crumbled into dust." He wants his work to be a testimony to his existence, "that the world may learn that there once lived such a man as Kah-ge-ga-gah-bowh, when they read his griefs and his joys."[20] Despite Krupat and Swann's assessment, Copway is "telling the whole of any one's individual life," rather than telling the story of his collective; he is also using "merely personal experience as of particular significance" to make his arguments, and it seems to be neither "foreign" nor "repugnant" to him. He warmly embraces the notion that his personal experience, his recollections, will live on after his death. One explanation might be that Copway has absorbed Western concepts and values. Cheryl Walker, author of *Indian Nation: Native American Literature and Nineteenth-Century Nationalisms*, concludes that his acculturation and subjugated discourse has deleterious effects:

> Some Native Americans, in the process of becoming literate, took to mimicking the discourse of the whites. But rather than stabilizing their position vis-à-vis the dominant culture, their rejection of their own heritage as often as not began a process of national

disestablishment that resulted, in the lives of the Indian authors themselves, in an almost complete loss of psychic balance. An example is George Copway ... [21]

Walker's explanation does not account for the idea that Copway's auto= biographical impulse, accompanied by his desire for fame, is not a rejection of his culture but rather is Ojibway, in that he is expressing his culture's value of actions that increase one's reputation and personal honour.[22] While Petrone is convinced that autobiography was foreign to Canada's "first literary coterie of Indians," she notes the influence of the oral tradition on the writings of Copway and his peers:

> Personal experiences were juxtaposed with communal legend and myth ... Despite their Christian and acculturated influence, their works are native accounts. *Aboriginal in origin, form, and inspiration*, their writings comprise the first body of Canadian native literature in English ... [23]

While Walker focuses on the assimilationist bent of nineteenth-century Christianized Indigenous writing, Petrone focuses on the ways in which they remain "native accounts."

Consider what comes from trying to determine the grounds for Copway's production of his life story. Perhaps Copway is colonialism's mimic man; or even in a less extreme reading, he is acculturated, assimilating a Western concept of self; or perhaps he is the opposite, schooled in and reproducing writing marked by his Anishinaabe identity. Any of these interpretations reveal our investment in defining Indigenous identity as essentially different from the Western standard. To be clear, I am not trying to diminish discussions about the effects of colonization or the influence of oral tradition or Indigenous epistemologies. But discussions such as those of Krupat and Swann, Walker and Petrone, equate particular forms or genres with authentic "Indian" identity. It is one thing to identify a literary tradition that some Indigenous writers draw upon and consider the cultural influences embedded in the art; it is quite another to suggest that the degree of influence by Euroamerican culture can measure either the writer's "authenticity" or (as with Walker) his "psychic balance." Particularly in discussions about Indigenous literatures, questions about literary form often collapse into discussions of Indigenous identity. The problem with defining and codifying Native American literary aesthetics as, for example, holistic, cyclical, and humorous is that this often deteriorates into defining the Native American as spiritual, nonhierarchical, and funny. These identity checklists are not only prescriptive and oppressive but are also unable to account for the diversity and range of writers or the creativity of their works that exceeds our expectations.[24]

My contention that Indigenous authors write autobiographically as a continuation of varying Indigenous intellectual traditions challenges Krupat's key premise that "unlike traditional Native literature, the Indian autobiography has no prior model in the collective practice of tribal cultures."[25] Krupat contends that whether written with a white collaborator (what he categorizes as "Indian autobiographies") or solely by an Indigenous author (as "autobiographies by Indians") these works are bicultural and thus not traditional forms, but rather a consequence of contact with whites because "there simply were no Native American texts until whites decided to collaborate with Indians and make them."[26] In contrast to this notion that Indigenous autobiography—indeed, all Indigenous literary production—is necessarily "bicultural," I argue that we Indigenous authors have absorbed, adopted, and appropriated a myriad of styles, including European, and integrated them into our traditions in order to tell Indigenous stories. Krupat's categorizing of literacy and autobiography as "white" inventions while designating orality and "the communal self" as "Indian" only obscures the multiple and complex influences that have shaped the genre of Native American autobiography, including the influence of Indigenous intellectual traditions that continue to exist up to the present day.[27]

Instead, I contend that Indigenous cultures have long-standing literary traditions;[28] Indigenous autobiographies are not examples of a European literary genre that has mutated to adapt to the life stories of Indigenous authors, but are instead examples of vibrant, innovative Indigenous intellectual production.

For a variety of reasons, despite the excellent work of Indigenous scholars like Craig S. Womack, Greg Sarris, and Joanne DiNova,[29] among others, the governing assumptions of the first generation of scholars of Native American autobiography—that Indigenous people did not write about themselves, that autobiography is a European invention—continue to hold sway. For example, when Annette Angela Portillo problematizes the genre of autobiography in her 2017 monograph, she builds upon Krupat's assertion that "the European invention of autobiography, a self-written life, [is] 'marked by egocentric individualism, historicism and writing,' [and] does not characterize Native American culture."[30] This reliance on Krupat's definition is troubling because Indigenous subjectivity is then limited to being Europe's "other." If European autobiography is supposedly marked by "egocentric individualism," the presumption is that Indigenous people are communal, with no room to discuss Indigenous values of personal choice, autonomy, independence, and self-reliance;[31] likewise the definition of autobiography as reliant on "historicism and writing," and therefore European, assumes that Indigenous discourse is based on the oral alone. This binary that conceives of Indigenous discourse as primarily oral and European discourse as primarily literary is a false divide that ignores the complex reliance of all cultures on a spectrum of literacies. It also gives the European chauvinist the justification to ignore Indigenous literary production, reifying the false binary between the spoken and the written.[32] Moreover, it distracts us from acknowledging the dismal access that Indigenous authors historically have had to publication. While this book primarily recognizes the impact of nêhiyawi-itâpisinowin on Cree and Métis literatures, it is impossible to discuss Indigenous literatures in Canada without also noting the crippling effects that the publishing and editing industry have had on all Indigenous literary production.

And in case the reader might think that some of the academic debates about Native American autobiographies articulated in the 1980s might no longer be relevant, I provide evidence that Krupat's assertion that autobiography is a European invention still has currency. In the 2020 edition of *The Routledge Handbook to the Culture and Media of the Americas*, Maryemma Graham and Mercedes Lucero sketch out the history of lifewriting in this hemisphere and begin with Saint Augustine's *Confessions*, circa 400 AD, as a model for spiritual autobiographies of Puritan New Englanders; they then discuss the adaptation of the fictional Bildungsroman to narratives about immigration and nation-building in the United States. To justify this focus on non-Indigenous writing, Graham and Lucero cite Daniel P. Shea, who argues that "*autobiography at first had no America*, and thus emerged to give focus to the imaginings of Anglo-European settlers"[33] (my emphasis). When Graham and Lucero introduce autobiographies by Indigenous authors like William Apess and Zitkála-Šá,[34] they emphasize that Native American authors embrace the written tradition only "for strategic purposes ... to draw attention to the plight of their people and the injustices they faced."[35] My work sits in opposition to these assumptions.[36] I argue that autobiographies by Indigenous authors—in many forms—exist as an Indigenous intellectual tradition; as such, Indigenous autobiography exists not just as a response to colonizers about injustice but also as an expression of specific culturally informed values and ideas to be shared with community members, descendants, and future generations.

Thus, it is possible not only to recognize Christian and Western conventions in Copway's life narrative, but also to acknowledge its Anishinaabe conventions without being drawn into discussions of cultural contamination or authenticity. Historian Michael Angel, in *Preserving the Sacred: Historical Perspectives on the Ojibwa Midewiwin*, lists the ways in which Ojibwa people have traditionally identified themselves:

If pre-contact members of the Ojibwa had been asked how they identified themselves, they would have replied that they were Anishinaabeg, the "First or True People" ... If asked to identify themselves more narrowly, members of the Anishinaabeg would have referred to small kinship or clan groups to which they belonged, since this was the most significant social group in Anishnabe society. Perhaps they would have referred to the name of the socio-economic unit or band to which they belonged. This name might be taken from the name of the leader, from the geographical location, or perhaps from the name of the clan in cases where all members were from the same clan.[37]

Angel's priorities of introduction and affiliation apply to Copway's text. Once Copway has assured his readers that he has converted to Christianity, and shared his aspirations for immortality, he introduces his family. He generally follows the stages that Angel proposes, first describing his parents as "of the Ojebwa nation," and then locating them more specifically "on the lake back of Cobourg, on the shores of Lake Ontario, Canada West."[38] He introduces his parents, describing his father as a medicine man and a good hunter, noting that because "no one hunted on each other's ground," his father's hunting territory was "the northern fork of the river Trent,[39] above Bellmont lake."[40] Copway then switches to discuss his great-grandfather, who was the first to enter the area to secure this hunting territory "after the Ojebwa nation defeated the Hurons," and notes that he was of the Crane totem or clan. His mother, "a sensible woman," was "of the Eagle tribe."[41]

This Anishinaabe convention, to introduce oneself by introducing one's nation, family, and territory, lives on in a modified form. When, in 2013, Lindsay Keegitah Borrows writes that "Anishinabeg Stories take [her] home," she explains that her "family history teaches [her] ways to articulate the legal, ceremonial, and intellectual stories of [her] community."[42] For this point, she cites the stories told to her by her grandmother as well as the family history written by her father, legal scholar John Borrows. And contemporary Anishinaabe researcher Kathleen Absolon identifies the starting point in Indigenous research practice to be "Locating My Self in My Search."[43]

Indigenous authors from many nations write autobiographically because it is in keeping with their nation's worldview.[44] In 1990, Emma LaRocque credits the role of Cree-Métis epistemology, "which does not separate the word from the self,"[45] blended with her feminist understanding of language, for the subversive use of her own voice, recognizing that this challenges the value of objectivity. She writes:

As a scholar, I am expected to remain aloof from my words; I am expected to not speak in my voice. But I am a Native woman writer/ scholar engaged in this exciting evolution/revolution of Native thought and action ... as an integrated person, I choose to use my own voice whether I am writing history or whether I am writing poetry.[46]

LaRocque links positioning her self in her writing with being able to "speak in [her] voice." Writing "as an integrated person," drawing on one's own auto-biography, is an Indigenous value.[47]

It is with these affirmations of autobiography as an Indigenous intellectual tradition, and the assertion that George Copway's autobiographical impulse is Anishinaabe in character, that I approach the later work by Swampy Cree Anglican minister James Settee [born 1809-died 1902].[48] Kristina Fagan Bidwell identifies Settee, along with Charles Pratt, as "an important part of the Cree literary tradition."[49] She identifies both Settee and Pratt as the "earliest Cree Writers in Saskatchewan" and notes that Settee kept detailed journals his entire life. Bidwell examines Settee's short story, "An Indian Camp at the Mouth of Nelson River Hudsons Bay," that he wrote in the late 1880s; while Settee hoped that it would be published in his lifetime, it was not published until 1977 when historian Jennifer Brown included it as part of published conference proceedings. "An Indian Camp" begins with the date, 1823, and continues:

On the latter end of September, my grand Father wished [to go] to the spot where he was born at the mouth of Nelson River. We was at Split Lake where my grand Father had settled and made a home [for] his old age.... My father got leave to take grand father down to the sea. We embarked in a Bark Canoe & followed the stream, saw plenty deer, geese, bears &c. but did not mind them, [as] we had enough provision. We saw a large Camp.

Settee then relates what it was that he saw and the stories he heard at this "pow-wow," at this "Feast," creating what Bidwell calls an "exceptional piece of writing ... [that] ought to be considered a founding work of prairie literature.[50]

"An Indian Camp" has been available to interested readers since 1977, and in 2018 was anthologized in Jesse Rae Archibald-Barber's *kisiskâciwan: Indigenous Voices from Where the River Flows Swiftly*, which includes historic Indigenous writers in what is now called Saskatchewan. Yet few have had the chance to read a different text, Settee's 7,000-word autobiography titled "Settee's Life," written in 1891 when he was about eighty years old. It was recently uncovered by historian Peter Geller, who is working on publishing it according to the wishes of Settee's community.[51] This autobiographical account is less overtly literary than "An Indian Camp," but both start at the same location. From the 1891 text, we understand that James Settee's grandfather did not originate in Split Lake, located in Manitoba's far north, but rather more than 200 kilometres east, at the mouth of the Nelson River:

> My first recollection when I was very young was at Split Lake in the Nelson River where my grandfather had made it his home. My father was in the Company's service as a guide transporting the supplies for the interior for the Northern Districts. The heathen world at that time [was] in a most degraded state. The baneful article [alcohol,] which had been introduced into the Country made them sevenfold more wicked than before, it was good a limited supply was given, if they had got what they wished they would have destroyed each other.

So, in the very first paragraph of his life story, Settee references social damage as the result of alcohol.

This resonates with Copway's account, which describes how the introduction of settlers to his territory at Rice Lake, in what is now called Ontario, coincided with the introduction of alcohol: "[My father], and others, became acquainted with the early settlers, and have ever been friendly with the whites; and I know the day when he used to shake the hand of the white man, and, *very friendly*, the white man would say "*take some whiskey*."[52] The result, according to Copway is that:

> The Ojibway nation, that nation unconquered in war, has fallen prey to the withering influence of intemperance ... The fire-water has rolled towards them like the waves of the sea. Alas, alas! My poor people! The tribe became dissipated, and consequently improvident, and often suffered intensely.[53]

The early part of the nineteenth century was a time of chaos for Copway's nation. He talks about the land-theft through treaties that his people signed, only to learn how to read and then discover they had been swindled. Copway writes: "But, since that time [in 1818 when land was surrendered to the British] some of us have learned to read, and to our utter astonishment, and to the everlasting disgrace of that *pseudo* Christian nation, we find that we have been most grossly abused, deceived, and cheated."[54]

Settee likewise describes his childhood as a difficult time for his people, emphasizing his hatred of intemperance and the fact that his family felt to be enough in danger from events Settee calls a "carousel" to warrant seeking safety from the Hudson's Bay Company Fort: "There were stockades around the building to keep our drunken Indians out of the houses."[55]

In Copway's autobiography, he links the rejection of alcohol with learning to read, which came with the added benefit of being able to use his literacy in English to criticize those who cheated his people. Settee adopts a similar circuit of ideas, stating that,

> ... tho' I saw the Indians every day I did not like their ways. I saw the Company's men sitting some days with their books in their hands, I was curious to know what they looked into their books for hours. My father had gone down to York Factory asking the Gentleman in Charge of the Fort to send down four Boats, and to bring me & three other boys to send up to Red River to school.[56]

Here Settee, already having established his hatred of intemperance, is intrigued by the act of reading and is sent to be one of the first students in the Missionary school. But intrinsically included in his education is Christian conversion. He writes that:

> The first night I came to St. John's School under the care of the Church Missionary Society, I was made to kneel down on my knees inside the Church and taught to say Great Father give me thy Holy Spirit for the sake of Jesus Christ our Lord, Amen. I did not understand what I said more than the cat is sitting on the table looking at my pen while I am writing.[57]

While Copway describes his dramatic Christian conversion in the middle of a thunderstorm, Settee's introduction to Christianity is comedic. In this vignette of himself in his old age, after having spent his adult life as a minister, Settee is looking at his cat while holding a pen in his hand—one of the implements that defined his career. The description of his boyhood conversion is meant to make us smile.

Settee embraces his lessons and becomes a minister, not with zeal to teach solely in the English language *per se*, but rather a zeal to teach reading and writing in whatever form. He describes work he conducted in Lac La Ronge in the 1840s:

> The Bible read every day the Indians would go and search their companions and bring them to me so that they might hear the word of God. The Indians was convinced of the truth stated in the Scripture. I taught the Children in English but the adults in their own

language. I made use of the Syllabics, which had been brought into use. I translated portions of Scriptures in syllabics and made the adults to learn them by heart. In the year 1848 our congregation increased to near 300 souls all baptized by my fellow labourer the late Venerable Archdeacon Hunter who was a most faithful Minister of Church.[58]

It could be tempting to follow the deductions of earlier scholarship such as that by Walker and conclude that, just as Copway was rejecting his culture as he embraced literacy and Christianity, so was Settee. To do so, however, ignores the fact that like Copway, Settee was living in a near-apocalyptic moment; previous Indigenous economic and governance systems were undermined by the encroachment of settlers and the usurpation of land. Food systems were failing. People were traumatized at a time when alcohol was being used as a trade good and being pressed upon Indigenous people. There was no way for Settee or other Cree people to choose "traditional heritage" that is separate from the invasion of the colonizers and separate from the economic and ecological destruction. Settee did not choose between traditional Cree ways of living and European Christianized ways; instead, he rejected the toxicity of despair to find a way to continue, just as nêhiyawak have always done.

Likewise, writing has always been enthusiastically embraced by nêhiyaw people. In her 2021 essay about Indigenous literacies, Métis art historian Gloria Jane Bell discusses the role and popularity of writing by Cree people prior to the confederation of Canada, as evidenced by the quick uptake of presses and the subsequent publication of Cree language materials, "including Cree language dictionaries, hymnals, and other paper works, during the mid-nineteenth century."[59] Bell explains that, in 1853, the Church Missionary Society sent a single-pull Albion printing press to Moose Factory in James Bay to be operated by Anglican Bishop James Horden.[60] She argues that, because there were so "many Cree language books [that] were printed by the press, ... there must have been a substantial community of Cree readers and speakers in the James Bay area and throughout Rupert's Land."[61]

Settee also affirms that writing and reading were embraced by Cree people. In a conversation with geologist and ethnologist Dr. Robert Bell, at the end of the nineteenth century, Bell asks Settee about the existence of books among the Cree prior to contact with Europeans. Settee replies that,

the Indian manuscript is as what I said before like the Hebrew Bible. Beginning the top page at the right hand & downwards to the left.

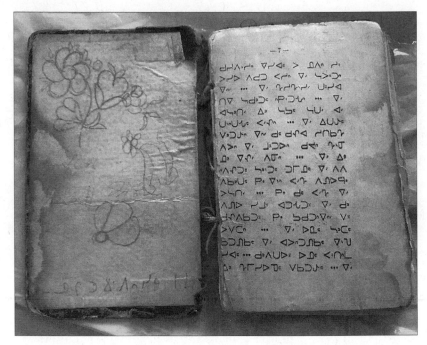

Fig. 3 câpân's prayerbook. Reprinted with permission by the Patterson family.

The Crees and the Saulteaux kept this manuscript but since [our missionaries] introduced books into the hands of the Indian the old way of writing is set aside. Those I have seen were among the Indians down in the Hudson Bay, and among the Saulteaux at the Gulf of St. Lawrence in Lower Canada.[62]

This is similar to Winona Stevenson (now Wheeler)'s assertion, in her 2000 article "Calling Badger and the Symbols of the Spirit Language: The Cree Origins of the Syllabic System," which contends that Wesleyan Methodist Reverend James Evans ought not to be credited with the creation of the Cree syllabary; instead, oral histories preserve the fact that the Cree writing systems predated contact.

In addition to this point, there is ample evidence that other forms of writing long preceded contact. As Stevenson notes, "age-old petroglyphs abound in Cree territory, especially in the Canadian Shield area around Stanley Mission."[63] All of this adds to the assertion that nêhiyawak value literacy, and have always valued literacy, so that its adoption should not be attributed to assimilation to dominant settler culture. The ability of nêhiyawak to adapt to new circumstances is not a sign of being conquered, but rather a sign of resilience and strength.

This reminds me that it was often said among family that kôhkom could read and write in syllabics, and some relatives remember that she kept her recipes for her medicines in a notebook. I know that her mom, my câpân, could read syllabics because my cousin Joanne has her bible. On the inside cover of the prayer book, you can see that câpân has been doodling. My friend suggested that she was likely trying to figure out a beading pattern. In the middle—in faint script—you can see her signature, with her married name from her second husband: Mrs. H. Morin. And on the very bottom she has written the date in syllabics: nôcihitowi-pîsim, the mating moon, also known as September.

kahkiyaw kiwâhkômitonaw

We are all related

CHAPTER TWO

Interrelatedness and Obligation
wâhkôhtowin in Maria Campbell's âcimisowin

The most famous autobiography, the most influential âcimisowin, by any Indigenous author in Canada, is hands down Maria Campbell's *Halfbreed*, first released in 1973 and now a classic. Yet even though as a child I knew the title of Campbell's book, I more easily associated it with "Half-Breed," a 1973 hit by Cher, whose variety show played on television weekly. I realize now that when I was growing up, I described my mother's side of the family as Cree, mostly because this was Mom's first language and the language she would speak to her brothers and sisters. I used the term Cree to avoid other terms my mother used, like "Indians," and especially "halfbreeds," which I thought was a racial slur used with a self-deprecating humour typical in my family. And as a child of the public school system in the 1970s and '80s I never learned any other terminology.

I knew about Métis politics, or as Auntie Irene and Uncle Frank pronounced it, "may-tiss" politics, because they told me about their involvement in the trip they took to Europe as part of a delegation in April 1981. It seemed to me that only people from Saskatchewan ever pronounced Métis as "maytiss."

I also have family that are Status Cree, although many of us grew up scattered around prairie cities like Edmonton or Prince Albert or Saskatoon, and so when I was growing up, the differences between Métis and Status Indians were not apparent to me.[1]

Uncle Frank's dad was Pete Tomkins, one of the "Famous Five" Métis activists who, along with Malcolm Norris, James Brady, Joseph Dion, and Felix Callihoo, established the Métis Association of Alberta in the 1930s. But this did not signify to me a stable identity: I came to understand that what kind of *Native* you are can shift. Uncle Frank's first wife had been Status before her marriage to him, and his grandmother was Poundmaker's widow. According to the rules of the Indian Act in 1876 that remained in effect until 1985,[2] any Status Indian woman who married a non-Status man would lose her Status, which is to say that her name would be erased from the registration lists of "Indians" recognized by the Canadian government. It didn't matter if the man was non-Indigenous or a Cree-speaking, moose-hunting, Indigenous rights activist who lived in the bush. If that man did not have Status, then the Status woman who married him would lose the rights she was entitled to because of the rules of the Indian Act. If she stayed single, or if she had a husband with a Status card, she would continue to have the rights (and burdens) of Status. This was the gender inequality that women fought, resulting in an amendment to the Indian Act in 1985, called Bill C-31, that allowed women who had lost their rights to apply to regain them for themselves and their children.[3]

At some point after Bill C-31 passed, each of Uncle Frank's children qualified to regain the Status lost to them when their mother married their father. Eventually, Frank applied under Bill C-31 for Status and was also granted membership in Poundmaker Cree Nation. This didn't negate his identity as Métis through his father's side, but instead recognized the history and rights of his own mother—Isobel Tomkins had been Status before she married Pete Tomkins Junior. Sometimes I hear debates that you can be Status or that you can be Métis and that you can't be both. I wonder about all the people I know who have both a Status and a Métis parent. I think about my conversations with my friend and mentor, Jo-Ann Episkenew, who passed in 2016. I remember her talking about her four children from her two marriages, two of whom are Status and two of whom are Métis. She was the one who explained the registration process, which indicates that you must identify as one or the other. "Why," she asked me, "should my two status kids have to give up claim to their Métis side?" I've often wondered about that. Why do they have to choose?

Robert Innes, author of *Elder Brother and the Law of the People*, argues that "[s]cholars have ... gone to great lengths to emphasize the differences and tensions between Métis and First Nations."[4] He points out that while not true in every case, relations between some First Nations and Métis communities were close, often due to a high rate of intermarriage. He notes, as an example, the fact that "Chief Poundmaker's mother was reputed to be Métis."[5]

Around 2005 I contacted an archive in Manitoba to gather information about my family genealogy. To my surprise, I noted that the scrip certificates—the documents Métis received in exchange for their resignation of treaty rights—made out to kôhkom's father, Cornelius Durocher, listed him not as Métis but as a Halfbreed, the word my mother used that I always thought was a racial epithet and not a legal category.[6]

While I haven't ever been comfortable using the term "halfbreed," for a long time I also wasn't comfortable describing myself as Métis because many of the symbols of Métis culture had no resonance in the life of our family. In my childhood I never saw a Métis sash or flag, never saw anyone play the fiddle or jig, and never heard Michif, as our family spoke Cree.[7] In a 2006 article, Brenda Macdougall explains how the "notion that a singular Métis consciousness and national identity emerged at Seven Oaks in 1817 is still widely accepted without question and continues to be the standard by which all Métis communities are judged, regardless of their own historical trajectories."[8] She cites the influence of the work of Marcel Giraud that emphasized southern Plains-based Métis society.[9]

Macdougall's contribution to the field is her focus on communities farther north; she also tries to avoid the "simplistic conclusions that the Métis are a 'people-in-between,' hybrids torn between the world of their non-Native fathers and Indian mothers."[10] Inspired by the predominance of Cree spoken in the area, she borrows the Cree cultural concept of wâhkôtowin that values the interconnections of family, place, and economic reality. Focusing on the core families from Île à la Crosse, Macdougall argues that this community was functionally matrilineal:

> Importantly, each of these generations reinforced socio-cultural patterns established in the late eighteenth century when the first wave of outsider male trade employees entered northwestern Saskatchewan and began establishing relationships with Cree and Dene women. More precisely, the women indigenous to the region became the centrifugal force incorporating successive waves of outsider males who carried with them the surnames that came to mark northwestern Saskatchewan communities and identified the families locally and patronymically. Aboriginal women—Cree, Dene, and then Métis—grounded their families in their homelands, creating for them a sense of belonging to the territory through a regionally defined matrilocal residency pattern and, therefore, female-centred family networks.[11]

I appreciate Macdougall's attempt to rethink fur trade history as more than the corporate history of the Hudson's Bay Company or the record of men who worked for it.[12] I also recognize my own family in her description of female-centred family networks. But this is not the only thing I recognize. When I read the names of core Métis families at Île à la Crosse that she lists, I see names of some of my ancestors: Josephte Durocher, Basile Meraste,[13] Abraham Laliberté, Serazine Morin.

Fragments of these names were embedded in my mother's stories and were listed clearly in the names of family members. And you had to pay attention. My câpân, my grandmother's mother, was born a Merasty, became a Durocher, and then after my great-grandfather's murder in 1913, remarried. Yet even though she became a Morin through marriage, because she knew her genealogy, she did not marry a cousin.[14]

The knowledge of family lines is a long-held value in Indigenous communities that precedes the recent explosion of interest in genealogical websites. As Tasha Beeds reminds us: "The first words often given by nêhiyawak (Cree and Cree-Métis people) and other Indigenous peoples articulate kinship and territory connections, placing introductions within the web of wâhkôtowin."[15] This knowledge identifies who nêhiyawak have obligations to as well as determines who was available as a marriage partner (or perhaps it is more accurate to state, who one is related to, and hence who is not available to marry).

This practice of explaining who you are through your connections to your relations is evident in Campbell's *Halfbreed*; it is equal parts a consideration of the family tree and of Cree theory. When Campbell outlines her genealogy at the beginning of the book, she is honouring the bonds of wâhkôhtowin. As Métis scholar Jo-Ann Episkenew states in her own discussion of *Halfbreed*, "The Elders' acknowledgement of their kinship with the Métis is significant because relationships between relatives are sacred in Cree culture."[16] Episkenew then explains in the accompanying endnote that:

> In the Cree kinship system, extended family relationships are more important than blood relationships. All of Maria's mother's sisters, had she had any, would also be considered Maria's mothers; all of Grannie Dubuque's sisters would be Maria's grandmothers, and all her brothers would be Maria's grandfathers. Relatives are wealth.[17]

This value of and respect for relational bonds is key to the Cree value of kinship. Even though as readers we identify that in *Halfbreed* Maria has one mother and one father, we don't always appreciate that the extended family she grows up around are parental figures in their own right.

In her account, Campbell starts with Great Grandpa Campbell from Edinburgh, Scotland, a mean and jealous man who flogged his wife, Cheechum, in public and not long after died a mysterious death. Cheechum was "a Halfbreed woman, a niece of Gabriel Dumont," whose mother's people lived in what is now Prince Albert National Park: "Even though they were Indians they were never part of a reserve as they weren't present when the treatymakers came."[18]

Cheechum's son was Grandpa Campbell, whose wife, Grannie Campbell, "was a small woman with black curly hair and blue eyes ... a Vandal" whose family had been in the Rebellion. After Grandpa Campbell's death, and a failed attempt at the impossible task of homesteading, Grannie Campbell, her eldest son—who was Maria's father—and eight other children "joined other 'Road Allowance people.'"[19] As Campbell describes it, those Métis who lost the rights to their land became squatters, eventually building along road lines and crown lands where they would not be run off by newly arrived landowners. In this way, the Métis literally lived on the margins of society.

Conversely, Grannie Campbell's sister Qua Chich married Big John, who had come to Sandy Lake, to homestead and find a wife: "Some years later, when the treaty-makers came, he was counted in and they became treaty Indians of the Sandy Lake Reserve [now Ahtahkakoop Cree Nation] instead of Halfbreeds."[20] Here Campbell clearly demonstrates the vagaries of registration under the Indian Act. While it is not clear if Big John is Métis or from a different band or First Nation, he did not originate in Sandy Lake.[21]

Maria's father met and married her mother when he was eighteen and she was fifteen. She was the daughter of Pierre Dubuque, "a huge strong-willed Frenchman" and of Grandma Dubuque, "a treaty Indian woman ... raised in a convent."[22]

On one hand, the value of wâhkôhtowin is evident, as Campbell places herself within a dynamic number of relatives and stories. But on the other hand, Campbell also reveals the power of Canadian legislation to undermine the connections in her family. When Canada formed and went about segregating Aboriginal people onto reserves, there was no infallible mechanism that appropriately tagged every person and community. There were occasions, such as with Cheechum's mother in what is now Prince Albert National Park, when some Indigenous people were missed; and while they avoided segregation on a reserve, they also had no legal right to continue to live on their land, no access to the resources that fed them, and no compensation for their loss. Even though Campbell notes that her great-grandmother was so intimidating that the RCMP only once attempted, without success, to evict her from what was deemed then to be a national park, Cheechum's descendants no longer live on this land and have no legal claim to it.

In contrast, Grannie Campbell's sister, who was a "Halfbreed" by birth, married Big John; there is no indication where his people come from, but when he moved to Sandy Lake, he (and therefore his wife) were registered as Status Indians and made members of the Sandy Lake Reserve. The fact that Big John brought resources with him when he arrived at Sandy Lake ("he brought with him two yoke of oxen, and a beautiful saddle horse"), had good fortune with farming, and then had access to land through treaty, explains how Qua Chich could be "considered wealthy by our standards."[23] By comparison, her sister, Grannie Campbell, just like the other Road Allowance people, had "no pot to piss in or a window to throw it out."[24]

Legislation is also why Maria's Grandma Dubuque was a Status Indian woman until her marriage to a Frenchman, after which she was no longer allowed to live on reserve near her family. Although Campbell identifies Pierre Dubuque as French, even had he been a Métis or a Native American, Grandma Dubuque's situation would have been the same, because he would not be considered a Status Indian under the Canadian Indian Act. However, these same rules do not apply to Grandma Dubuque's brother, who like her was born a Status Indian but because of his gender as male, never lost it in adulthood; and even without any biographical detail, we know that Grandma Dubuque's brother's wife had Indian Status, regardless of her background because, under the rules of the Indian Act, a woman marrying a Status Indian would instantly receive Indian Status upon marriage, if she didn't have it before. The brother is never in danger of losing his status and he becomes "chief on his reserve."[25] In the story, it seems that during Maria's childhood, Grandma Dubuque is single; Campbell mentions that she lives in Prince Albert where she "cleaned for well-to-do families."[26]

This government-imposed system clearly undermined family ties, and it did so purposely—for one thing, the fewer Status Indians, the less the government had to spend in obligations. For example, while members such as Grandma Dubuque's brother and his family had the treaty-protected right to hunt for food, his sister did not, and likewise her daughter's family did not. Having been raised on the land and having a hungry family to feed, Danny Campbell defies the law and hunts, hiding the meat in an underground stash. When the RCMP pay a visit, they offer Maria a chocolate bar if she will tell them where he hides the game. When she "sells out" for an Oh Henry! bar, her father is taken to jail in Prince Albert for six months.[27] Not only is he criminalized for feeding his family, but without his help the family goes hungry: "We had no money and no meat."[28] It is not only identity that is legislated. Criminality and hunger are legislated. Although Campbell does not describe such a thing, had one of the members of the family who were treaty decided to share the food that they had hunted, they would likewise be subject to arrest, as any game caught by treaty Indians could not legally be shared with non-treaty people.[29]

Also, a spatial divide emerges in the family. The treaty Indians in the family were segregated to the reserves and, especially in the Prairie provinces until the end of World War II, prevented from leaving without a pass from the Indian agent.[30] On the other hand, women like Grandma Dubuque who lost their rights to live on reserve near family, often gravitated towards urban centres, where they could work as wage labourers to make a living. Even though during Campbell's childhood, families like Grannie Campbell's lived literally on the margins of society, on the road allowances, a generation later these settlements would be abandoned as members of Métis and non-status communities relocated to cities in order to find work.[31] Maria's departure from her community to Vancouver where she ended up working in the sex and drug trade is, in some ways, representative of Métis and non-Status Indian people, women in particular; when their vulnerable communities crumbled, often the only option was to move to poor sections of cities with limited economic opportunities.[32]

However, it would be wrong to identify Maria only as poor and her family only as vulnerable. In *Halfbreed*, Campbell describes the vitality in her community, the strength and the boisterous humour, all in the context of a devastating defeat of the Riel Resistance a few generations before. Yet this history is not forgotten. In fact, Campbell begins Chapter One as a correction to "history books [that] say that the Halfbreeds were defeated at Batoche in 1884." She recounts the history according to the Métis, including the fact that the federal government would not negotiate with Riel but rather spent millions to squash their claims; with Riel hanged, "the other Halfbreeds escaped to the empty pockets of North Saskatchewan" where she was born.[33]

The retelling of these histories is propelled, according to Neal McLeod, by the value of "wâhkôhtowin [that] keeps narrative memory grounded and also embedded within the life stories of individuals."[34] The result is, according to McLeod, Cree narrative memory, which is "storytelling grounded in history, cultural understanding and personal relationships ... it is a mix of interpretation and description ... blend[ing] recounting and explanation."[35]

The value of wâhkôhtowin and the enaction of Cree narrative memory is evident when Maria learns Métis history from her Cheechum. In what Campbell calls her "first real lesson" in her life, she describes an episode as a child in which she and her siblings are taunted at school because of their poverty. When the young Maria gets home, she lashes out at her parents out of anger and internalized hatred: "I kicked her and said that I hated her, Daddy, and 'all of you no-good Halfbreeds.'"[36] Cheechum subsequently takes Maria into the woods and, before she disciplines her, gives her a detailed account of the injustices her community had suffered, leaving their homes to move west, sacrificing wealth for freedom from domination under a white supremacist state, only to face loss at Batoche. But rather than unite in resistance to a common enemy, some discontented Métis internalized the messages of racism and the indignities of poverty, to complain to each other that "you no-good Halfbreeds are ruining it for me,"[37] the same complaint that Maria had made of her parents. Cheechum uses history to warn Maria about how those in power exploit this sense of self-hatred: "The white man saw that that was a more powerful weapon than anything else with which to beat the

Halfbreeds, and he used it and still does today. Already they are using it on you."[38] Cheechum is teaching Maria not to believe the messages of self-hatred but instead to recognize the harm they do to her as a person and to her community.

This is just one example that Campbell uses to demonstrate that shame is a form of psychological warfare used against her community. Campbell describes the poor self-esteem of her community's men who have internalized racist beliefs against them: "I never saw my father talk back to a white man unless he was drunk."[39]

In this teaching, Campbell is demonstrating the understanding of multiple perspectives that Cree-Métis philosopher Lorraine Brundige describes as embedded in Cree philosophy. Cheechum teaches Maria that she needs to be aware that she is susceptible to the negative opinions from others and that she needs to fight against these consciously; she needs to be responsible for her own perceptions.

Brundige asserts that Cree philosophy trains people to recognize both their own perceptions and the perceptions of others.[40] Because there is an understanding that everyone speaks from a different perspective, there is the need for perceptual reality checks and re-checks. This works in concert with the value of wâhkôhtowin, to negotiate relationships, and both are evident in Cree narrative memory that refuses to act as a metanarrative but instead is responsive to listeners, contexts, place, and time. When the Cree first began to interact with Europeans, according to Brundige, they understood that Europeans had a different worldview, but that it was important to share their land in order to "come together in a relationship as relatives who had much to learn and benefit from each other."[41] Responsibilities to those you are in relationship with underlie everything.

In order for the value for wâhkôhtowin, the interrelatedness of all things, and the value for multiple perspectives to function together, respect for various points of view must be demonstrated to ensure that subsequent social, economic, and cultural exchanges are reciprocal, for the mutual benefit of all involved. Should any one person or group refuse to submit to these protocols, the system breaks down. McLeod writes about the obligations inherent in this worldview: "people tell stories to other people who are part of the stories and who will assume the moral responsibility to remember."[42]

But this is the vulnerability of the system. If people refuse to listen, or refuse to consider they have obligations to their neighbours, then the system collapses. For example, when the white community does not respect Métis people, wâhkôhtowin is effectively rejected. The only solution is the remedy Cheechum shares with Maria: to refuse the messages of self-hatred and to fight against them through community loyalty and self-respect.

Cheechum also has another tactic to fight against the incursions and disrespect of dominant society. While the Cree value of wâhkôhtowin requires obligations towards kin, Cheechum feels no obligation to be in relationship with settlers. Her policy is one of non-compliance. She understands that the only way to defy the hegemony that infiltrates every aspect of Métis life is an absolute refusal to interact with white society. She does not sleep on a bed or eat at a table.[43] When she meets settlers who have built on Indigenous lands, she ignores them and refuses to acknowledge them even when passing on the road.[44] When her grandson wants to enlist, Cheechum "was violently opposed to the whole thing and said we had no business going anywhere to shoot people, especially in another county. The war was white business, not ours, and was just between rich and greedy people who wanted power."[45] She understands that the poverty of the Métis is created by the arrival and settlement of whites, and she sees how it is connected to imperialism internationally.

Likewise, Cheechum understands how cultural hegemony functions—the adoption of values that benefit the ruling class to the detriment of a less powerful group's revolutionary goals. When Maria becomes upset about their family poverty and insults her parents, Cheechum metes out punishment with a searing critique of white Canadian society: "they try to make you hate your people."[46] Understanding the mechanisms of how this works, she refuses to have her picture taken by "two white-haired ladies ... wearing two-piece bathing suits."[47] Cheechum refuses to cede power. She knows not to submit to being made a spectacle so that her image would become a photograph outside of her control. Her response is to cover her head with her shawl and refuse to respond.

On another occasion when the family goes to a film about the Riel Rebellions, Maria is horrified to see her Métis heroes "made to look like such fools" while the North West Mounted Police and General Middleton "did all the heroic things."[48] While others were willing, Halfbreeds included, to stay and laugh hysterically, "Cheechum walked out in disgust."[49] She understood how powerful the use of images is in influencing how people or communities saw themselves.

For Cheechum the only answer was complete non-participation. She refused to convert to Christianity. She scorned welfare and even her old age pension, insisting that she should try her best to be self-sufficient.[50] For her, pride was also a protection. At one point when Maria begins to understand that she and her family are not welcome in town, she refuses to walk as though she were ashamed. Cheechum heartily endorses this: "Never forget that, my girl. You always walk with your head up and if anyone says something then put out your chin and hold it higher."[51] Cheechum opposes welfare,

Christianity, and schools, to her all arms of the government, because they erode personal self-esteem and self-reliance. Campbell describes her philosophy: "My Cheechum used to tell me that when the government gives you something, they take all you have in return—your pride, your dignity, all the things that make you a living soul. When they are sure that they have everything, they give you a blanket to cover your shame."[52]

When Campbell tries to get off the streets she moves to Calgary, and before she has a chance to get work, she needs money to feed her small children. She is coached by her roommate to "act ignorant, timid and grateful" and arrive at the welfare office wearing a "threadbare red coat, with old boots and a scarf" dressed up to look like the stereotype of what a poor, needy "Indian" woman would look like.

> [The social worker] insisted that I go to the Department of Indian Affairs, and when I said I was not a Treaty Indian but a Halfbreed, he said if that was the case I was eligible, but added, "I can't see the difference—part Indian, all Indian. You're all the same." I nearly bit my tongue off sitting there trying to look timid and ignorant.[53]

After suffering this racist tirade, she is given financial assistance but warned not to waste government money. According to Cree values, Campbell was wealthy because she had a lot of family, and as a descendent of original inhabitants on the Prairies she also, by rights, should have had some benefit from the economic prosperity built on land stolen from her and Indigenous people. Instead, she is forced to beg and treated as though she deserves disrespect.

At this point in the narrative, Campbell has run away from her family and struggles with addiction and numerous failed romances. She has made a living through illegal activities. However, it is only after going to the welfare office that she discusses a sense of shame. She says, "I left his office feeling more humiliated and dirty and ashamed than I had ever felt in my life."[54] She tells her friend that she would rather work on the street than have to return to welfare.

As much as Campbell is unwilling to humiliate herself, turning down a chance to work "dressed up as an Indian" for the Calgary Stampede, she knows that she has been vulnerable to messages from white society and has internalized shame of herself and of her people. She knows that she wears the blanket that Cheechum warned her about: "I don't know when I started to wear it, but it was there and I didn't know how to throw it away."[55] Even when she is involved in activism and politics, she still struggles because she does not know how to be free of it. In one of her final visits with Cheechum, Maria tells her that she is working at a halfway house for women, not to solve their personal problems but to offer shelter and friendship. Cheechum approves: "Each of us has to find himself in his own way and no one can do it for us. If we try to do more, we only take away the very thing that makes us a living soul. The blanket only destroys, it doesn't give warmth."[56] Taking over someone's autonomy under the guise of charity is one way to understand what Cheechum refers to as "the blanket." But Cheechum also considered scrip to be such a pretext. When, during the Riel Resistance, the federal government issued land scrip to a chosen few, it caused "a split within the Halfbreed ranks."[57] This tactic of divide and conquer eroded the loyalty that lies at the core of Cree-Métis systems of obligation and threatened the collective.[58]

In the conversations that Maria has with Cheechum, Campbell describes their relationship as one between a young person and an Elder, as two people who see things differently. This demonstrates that everyone has his or her own perspective, that everyone tells stories, including their own story, from a different point of view. Lorraine Brundige describes this:

> Contrary to contemporary interpretations of communal versus individual rights, when social decisions were made by historical Swampy Cree, the people came together as a community, but each "individual" was recognized as having their own opinion (perception) and each person contributed to the discussion. Thus, individual rights (perceptions) and collective rights (perceptions) were brought together in relationship. No one person was thought to hold a truth above everyone else and everyone's perceptions were granted equal opportunity to be represented. Understanding the full implications of consensus can help in the process of relationship building that is both reciprocal and respectful.[59]

What is striking about this is that key to consensus and relationship building is personal autonomy.[60] Cheechum warns Maria of the pitfalls of *help* (as in charity) and *government bargains* (as in scrip) because you cede autonomy and therefore power and control. In Cree culture, autonomy and self-sufficiency were vital to healthy relationships, to wâhkôhtowin.

> Autonomy and self-sufficiency were always taught within the context of interconnectedness – respectful relationships with all living beings. It was not an act of selfishness, but rather the development of skills, knowledge and capacity of the individual, so that they can enhance the capacity and strength of the web of relationships.[61]

Underlying the values of interrelatedness and multiple perspectives is the common reference point of shared narratives and memories that emphasize cooperation. This is the vision that raises the hopes of Campbell's father when he tries to work with Malcolm Norris and James Brady to improve the living conditions of their community. The gains in Alberta in the 1930s, after all, were made because of these shared values, narratives, and memories. But But in the community organizing in Saskatchewan in the 1950s, sabotage came from the government when only some of the members were given advantages akin to bribes, "and this had caused much fighting among our people, and had divided them."[62]

Campbell discovers that it is only in reclaiming the Cree value of wâh-kôhtowin, which considers family relationships to be sacred and obligations between kin to be immense, that she can discard this blanket of self-hatred and internalized racism. In this way Campbell states that she has "brothers and sisters, all over the country." Her vision is inclusive, no longer restricted to "an armed revolution of Native people." Instead, by sharing her story with her readers she gives them an opportunity, the obligation, to unite with her to "fight our common enemies," those who continue to ignore the suppression of Indigenous people, both historically and in the present day. Her final sentence speaks to her return to the values of her people as taught to her by Cheechum; her final words are "I no longer need my blanket to survive."[63]

Campbell wrote this resounding concluding statement in her âcimisowin. It is a statement of courage and confidence, much like the announcement in her introduction: "I write this for all of you, to tell you what it is like to be a Halfbreed woman in our country."[64] This is not just a book for a Métis readership. She publicly addresses "all of you" because she wants every one of her readers, everyone in Canada, to participate in her story even if they do not know the history.

> Going home after so long a time, I thought that I might find again the happiness and beauty I had known as a child. But as I walked down the rough dirt road, poked through the broken old buildings and thought back over the years, I realized that I could never find that here. Like me the land had changed, my people were gone, and if I was to know peace I would have to search within myself.[65]

It is at that precise time when she decided to look within herself to find peace that she decided to write about her life. While Campbell stated that she originally wrote a long letter to herself, eventually a friend suggested to her that it was a book in the making. Only a published book could reach enough people to oblige her readers to understand Canada and themselves differently. In this way Campbell treats her audience like kin. This is why, at the end of the book, she admits that she no longer believes in "an armed revolution of Native people" because it would not achieve what she wants; "we would only end up oppressing someone else." Instead, she makes a prediction: "I believe that one day, very soon, people will set aside their differences and come together as one. Maybe not because we love one another, but because we will need each other to survive. Then together we will fight our common enemies."[66] Love is not the key ingredient to the bond in wâhkôhtowin. Essential to Cree ideas around kinship are intense loyalty and obligation.

However, even as Campbell is employing the principle of wâhkôhtowin to share her experiences, depending on the resulting loyalty and sense of obligation to persuade her readers to remember her story, during the publication of the book there is an absence that signifies a betrayal. A significant passage that Campbell had fought with her publishers to include was excised without her permission. She only discovers that the passage has been removed when her author's copies are delivered to her home in early 1973.

In her composition of *Halfbreed* Campbell discusses the callous treatment of her community by Church and State. However, Campbell also courageously authors a passage that tells of her rape at the age of fourteen by an RCMP officer. At the time of its occurrence, she had been at her home alone and when her grandmother returned, she told Maria not to say anything:

> Grannie was afraid that Dad would come home, so she helped me upstairs and put me to bed. She told me not to tell Daddy what had happened, that if he knew he would kill those Mounties for sure and be hung and we would all be placed in an orphanage. She said that no one ever believed Halfbreeds in court; they would say that I had been fooling around with some boys and tried to blame the Mounties instead.[67]

This devastating passage demonstrates Maria's lack of legal or social recourse at the time to speak about the rape or seek justice, compounding her inability to voice her anger and pain until it erupts in self-damaging ways.

The opportunity to write about this act of violence in her autobiography would finally give Campbell an outlet, requiring others—"all of you"—to listen and remember. It would allow the author to report a rape she was not permitted to talk about; it would allow her to share her story with other women who had been sexually assaulted but who had never reported out of fear they would be disbelieved. It would allow her to question society about the mechanisms that silence women, especially Indigenous women. But her editors would not allow it. Despite the assurances that Campbell had consulted a lawyer who had told her she could proceed with publication, the Press decided that the risk was too great and eliminated the passage.[68]

There is no way that she could have known that her autobiography would become a bestseller.[69] Had this passage not been removed, the effect is, of course, impossible to say. But all those innumerable readers who inherited the "moral responsibility to remember" didn't get the whole story.

In Harmut Lutz's 1991 *Contemporary Challenges*, he interviews Campbell and asks her if she would ever like to re-write *Halfbreed*. She responded:

> Yes, some day. I don't think I'd make changes. What I would do with the book is, I would only put in that piece that was taken out. I wouldn't want to touch what's there, because that was the way I was writing then, and I think that it's important it stays that way, because that's where I was at.[70]

In discussions with colleagues over the years, I know that several researchers have tried to find the passage.[71] In 2017, I and Alix Shield, at the time a graduate student at Simon Fraser University, had the great fortune to be seated next to Maria Campbell as part of a conference in Dublin, Ireland. While a hero of ours for a long time, by 2017 she had grown even greater in stature; I drew upon protocols that I have been taught, trying to bring up points in common, trying to follow her lead in case she didn't want to talk to us.

At first, I brought up relatives, people we knew in common, including my uncle and her nephew. Because she seemed genuinely interested in what we were doing, we brought up our questions about *Halfbreed* and possible locations of the original manuscript and stifled a gasp of horror when she speculated that she had likely burned the first, hand-written version. At the time, knowing that the final version was in the hands of the Press, she hadn't seen any reason to keep the rough draft.

Knowing that Alix was about to go for a month-long residency at the McClelland and Stewart archives in the Fall, we asked permission to carry on the search. Maria Campbell approved, although she didn't have much hope that after all these years anything still existed. She told us that, once *Halfbreed* was published and she realized the press had gone against her expressed wishes and removed her description of the sexual assault even though she insisted it remain, she had asked for the excised section to be returned to her; the Press told her that any copy they had that included this section had been destroyed.

In what is undoubtedly the find of the decade, Alix, during her visit to the archives, was able to locate and read through the typescript for *Halfbreed*, prepared for the copyeditors. Where others had been unsuccessful, Alix located the missing and long-missed passage.

In an effort to make sure that this text was returned to Campbell as its rightful owner, Alix and I worked together to do so in a good way. It was something we took seriously because, as amazing a find that Alix uncovered, the text was about a painful incident and we didn't want this return to cause any harm. From the time of Alix's discovery until we were able to return the text to Campbell, we were sensitive that while this was a great discovery, it was also likely a reminder of a series of injustices, a series of blows, and we didn't want to add to that in any way. It was because of our sense of wâh-kôhtowin that we knew that to add to any hurt of Campbell would only add to our own, and likewise her joy to our joy. A year later, Alix and I attended the Indigenous Literary Studies Association conference in Vancouver, where Maria was in conversation with her niece Nicola Campbell, and she shared a Cree concept, kwayaskwastâsowin (put things to right) with the crowd.[72] It became a central idea in Alix's doctoral work, and in fact is the title of her thesis, which she defended in 2020. When Campbell, along with Cree-Métis scholar Kim Anderson, worked with Penguin to have the book reissued in late 2019, this time with the missing passage finally reinstated, Alix and I felt that sense that things had been put to right.

âskaw mâna ayiwâk kîkway astêw âcimowinihk

Sometimes there's more to a story

CHAPTER THREE

Respectful Interaction and Tolerance for Different Perspectives

kihcêyihtamowin in Edward Ahenakew's *Old Keyam*[1]

One of my cousins and I were in La Ronge, Saskatchewan, talking together about our grandparents. Eric and I were sharing family stories, particularly about kôhkom's reputation as a healer. Our Uncle Vic was with us, and I retold the story of how kôhkom had healed Absolom Halkett from blindness, recounting her need to dream to find the remedy: kôhkom told Absolom to give her some time to think. At some point she fell asleep and had a dream that a bear was being choked by thin willow branches, twined around its neck. The bear kept tugging at them. When she woke up, kôhkom went out and collected the leaves she saw in the dream and used them to make a poultice. When Absolom returned, she told him to put the medicine on his eyes every night for three nights and to wash it off every morning. It worked, and he never did go blind.

What amazed me is that once I finished, Uncle Vic told us that while he knew this story, he had never heard about the dream. I was astonished. This was such a significant feature of every telling that I had ever heard that I couldn't imagine anyone leaving that part of it out.

A few years later my husband and I flew to Edmonton for my cousin Lindsay's wedding. I had the chance to visit with Uncle Vic again. Since the previous visit, I had checked in with Auntie Irene, his sister, and she had confirmed that she had heard the same version that I knew, that featured the dream. "How else, she had asked me, would kôhkom have known what medicine to give?"

"What I wonder," I told Uncle Vic, "was why you didn't know this part of the story. Why weren't you told?"

His response was really helpful. "What you don't understand is that we were told that the Indian stuff was no good and that the white man's things were better. I remember laughing at some medicine that Mom made, and my sister Bella got angry with me and told me that I had to believe. That she would say this, that really surprised me."

"But you know," he continued, "there were lots of things that happened that you wouldn't believe. Once Dave was canoeing out on the lake and they figured he made someone angry by going too close to their campsite, so that when he came home one of his hands was limp. I remember the old ladies, my mom, her mom, and an old friend got together to figure out how to heal him. I remember them talking about it for quite a bit and then they started to work on him and they fixed his arm."

I was grateful for his stories and thanked him. I knew that in my mom's generation it was almost shameful to believe in "Indian ways." There was such a disregard for Cree ways of knowing and living, for nêhiyawêwin, for our history. It reminded me, as I studied the work of Anglican cleric and Cree scholar Edward Ahenakew, how resilient he would have to be, in the face of

Fig. 4 Vic Patterson, Thanksgiving 2005.

dismissal by the dominant culture that was certain of its superiority. And how radical Ahenakew was, to insist on the integrity and value of nêhiyaw perspectives.

Edward Ahenakew grew up in Saskatchewan, although a few generations before my mother and her siblings. He was born in 1885, a year that is referred to in Cree as either ê-kî-mâyahkâmikahk,[2] or kâ-mâyahkâmikahk, translated literally as "when it went wrong." It was a year of tremendous upheaval: the year of the North-West Rebellion, also known as the Riel Resistance—the same year that Louis Riel was hanged by Canada for high treason. As a result, Ahenakew was born into a family sequestered onto reserves, where the Cree language was still predominant, and he was sent to residential school, where he learned English. He was literate in both Cree and English and grew up in a home that had already embraced Christianity.

Ahenakew wrote at least three versions of his âcimisowin, his autobiography; all three are held in the Provincial Archives of Saskatchewan. The first is an eleven-page draft titled "The Story of the Rev. Canon Edward Ahenakew," where he writes about his life as part of a large, impressive family, focusing on his male relatives in his paternal line and including a few details about his childhood. The most evocative is about the moment he enters Residential School for the first time:

> With much trepidation I allowed myself to be handed over to the Principal of the School ... I shed no tears but the pain in my heart, as I looked at my father walking away, was great. He never looked back once. I was much depressed and did not even pay attention to a number of boys kicking a football around the grounds close by.[3]

His second example of âcimisowin is twenty-seven pages long, titled "Genealogical Sketch of My Family"; it was donated to the Boas Collection in 1948 and informed the publication of "The Story of the Ahenakews" published after his death by his editor Ruth M. Buck. In the 1948 version, he describes himself as "a weak, ailing baby"; he recounts an episode when he was so ill at the age of three that he could not eat until, after eleven days, a "girl-cousin of mine brought me a strawberry, the first ripe one found that summer"; the effect is that it seemed to "[remind] my stomach that it had work to do."[4] This is an intimate story of himself as a vulnerable child, cared for by a loving young relative. While he includes other short stories about his childhood, the majority of the narrative is about the lives of other family members.[5]

While the first two texts are straightforward examples of autobiography, they are short. His unpublished *Old Keyam* manuscript is longer, composed of over 168 handwritten pages, that is less a chronology of his life and more a mouthpiece for Ahenakew's unfettered opinions. It features a character—Old Keyam—who rejects mainstream success and goes about the community storytelling, sharing his opinions constantly. Ahenakew states:

> He will speak for himself in these pages and if we take the trouble to listen to what he says, perhaps we may see the viewpoint of many others like him who stand bewildered in the maze of things, not knowing exactly what to do but hiding their keen sense of defeat under an assumed demeanor of "keyam"[6] ie. "I do not care!"[7]

While Ahenakew's original has never been published in full, a curtailed version was released after Ahenakew's death as the second half of a book by editor Ruth M. Buck, under the title *Voices of the Plains Cree* (1973).

From Buck's notes we know that *Old Keyam*, while not perfectly polished, was begun in the 1920s and was completed. We also know from correspondence that he made several attempts to get this manuscript published, but remained unsuccessful.[8] After his death in 1961 his niece, Katie Ahenakew Greyeyes, gathered up his papers and entrusted them to Buck, whose parents had been missionaries on Ahenakew's home reserve.[9] Buck is to be credited for the great deal of work involved in the preparation of the manuscript and the efforts to contact potential publishers. After several attempts over the years to publish two of his works, she was able to combine two of them into one volume, the first half consisted of the stories Ahenakew had gathered from Chief Thunderchild in interviews held in the early 1920s and the second half included a shortened and edited version of his *Old Keyam* manuscript. The result is *Voices of the Plains Cree*, published first in 1973 with McClelland and Stewart, accompanied by Buck's nine-page introduction.[10]

Both versions, the unpublished *Old Keyam* manuscript and the second half of *Voices*, also called "Old Keyam," feature the story of a man—like Ahenakew—who is old enough to remember community members who lived on the land before encroachment and young enough to have attended residential school. Woven into the narrative is a montage of Ahenakew's sermons and lecture notes. For example, chapters 11 and 12 in the handwritten manuscript, titled "The Indian and the Great War" and "The League of Indians of Canada," draw from an address Ahenakew delivered on June 16, 1920 for the Annual Meeting of the Women's Auxiliary in Prince Albert, Saskatchewan. In this address Ahenakew responds to the essay by Duncan Campbell Scott, "The Indians and the Great War," published as part of the 1919 Annual Report of the Department of Indian Affairs. Ahenakew, like Scott, celebrates the enthusiastic involvement of Status Indians in the First World War, a conflict that they had no obligation to enter as non-citizens (they were classified as "wards of the state"). Ahenakew, like Scott, also commends the Indian bands and individuals who donated to the war effort, including "[o]n many reserves, especially down East, the women [who] formed Red Cross Societies or Patriotic Leagues."[11]

But the two have opposing goals: Duncan Campbell Scott celebrates the assimilating power of military service. He writes: "The return of so many Indian soldiers who have been broadened and inspired by contact with the outside world and its affairs is bringing about radical and progressive changes in the life of the reserves."[12] Scott then lists new amendments of the Indian Act that detail compulsory enfranchisement and erode First Nations mineral and logging rights. By contrast, Ahenakew uses this lecture, and his references to Indigenous participation in the war effort, to argue for increased Indigenous rights, improved access to education, and the value of political organizing of Indian bands across Canada; as part of his lecture, he promotes an upcoming 1920 League of Indians conference in Manitoba.

To incorporate this lecture as well as the goals of the League into the larger unpublished *Old Keyam* manuscript, Ahenakew modifies his words, from the first person in his lecture to a monologue spoken by Old Keyam, the character he creates. In an address to his community, Old Keyam discusses the Preamble to the League of Indians Constitution clause by clause, and refers to the need to: foster regular meetings and a national "brotherly relationship" among other First Nations; uphold high regard for Indigenous people and to "dissipate the erroneous opinions prevalent, that the Indian is necessarily incapable and a mere child"; urge First Nations to continue to be law-abiding citizens, loyal to the British Crown, respectful of the war dead, disabled soldiers, and war widows and families; and demand improved education and hygiene standards. And also:

> To abide steadfastly by the principle, that, inasmuch as Indians throughout the Dominion have rendered substantial and willing service in the cause of humanity, it becomes our privilege and right, as a distinctive race and native nationality of Canada, to claim better recognition at the hands of Parliament, in respect to more equality in privileges and opportunity as citizens and subjects of the British Crown.[13]

And then Keyam ends this speech with the following comment: "I have given the idea in my own words. You can think it out for yourselves."[14] This rhetorical move at the end of this speech reflects Cree values of personal autonomy that prizes persuasion rather than coercion; Old Keyam explicitly states that the audience can think through the complex issues independently.

Ahenakew's editor, Ruth M. Buck, points out that the character of Old Keyam and the work of the same name were highly personal to its author.[15] She states:

> The manuscript, in fact, represented a painful and even hazardous process of thought for Ahenakew ... Much of the material is drawn from his own experiences in the counselling of his people, and is sometimes autobiographical. It expresses his deep concern for his people, but it reveals also the humour and understanding that won friendship for him wherever he went, and made it possible for him to accept rebuffs, and that enlivened his calm stoicism.[16]

When Buck mentions that writing was a "hazardous process," she is pointing out that speaking his own mind was not without risk. As a Status Indian and a cleric, Ahenakew was not free to participate in any activity he wished. For example, in 1933 he was forced to give up his position in the League of Indians for Western Canada: "the Indian Department urged the bishop to tell him to attend to his duties as a churchman and not meddle in the affairs of the state."[17]

But the term "hazardous process" also marks the restrictions Ahenakew lived under and the complexities that he negotiated. Canon Ahenakew's position was particularly conflicted as well as scrutinized. It was difficult for Ahenakew, bilingual and literate in both Cree and English, a Status Indian and cleric, a Cree and a Christian, to express his opinions and experiences. Buck states that "in 1923 ... withdrawal was the only alternative if an Indian could not agree to Government or Church policy, and Edward Ahenakew knew that well."[18]

Yet Ahenakew does not withdraw; instead, he creates a character who seems to withdraw but who is actually very engaged in the debates of his day. In Chapter One of his original manuscript, titled "Old Keyam an 'Old Man' of the Band," he writes:

> It was here [on the reserve] that Old Keyam plied his trade, poor, inoffensive and genial. All the children loved him while the older people welcomed his approach. Though he was not very much above middle-age, he acted as the "Old Man" of the Reserve. Having lived with a missionary while yet a boy, he was able to speak English and could read and write. It is said that he had for a time done well for himself as a young man, but that he had suddenly allowed himself to slacken. He would not work, and everything he had soon evaporated into nothing. Some said it was because of disappointment in love, others said that Keyam had some words with the Indian Agent;

whatever it was he ceased to work and to care. He adopted the old Indian outlook on life, he allowed his hair to grow long and began to go from house to house in the evenings, building up for himself a reputation as a story-teller.[19]

In this sketch, cut short in Ruth M. Buck's version, Ahenakew explains the difficult position of his age group. He laments the passing on of the previous generation and proposes that Old Keyam is their successor "who looks not only to the past but who attempts, however feebly, to look at the future."[20]

In the second half of *Voices of the Plains Cree*, edited by Buck, there are passages that have sudden and contradictory shifts. The character, Old Keyam, speaks with the fire of a Cree activist and then he preaches submission to government and church authority. Maria Campbell and Cree historian Winona Wheeler discuss the second half of *Voices of the Plains Cree*, titled "Old Keyam," and argue that many of the passages are addressed to non-Aboriginal readers "who have the power to address ineffective and harmful federal Indian policies"[21]; however, embedded in the text are coded messages designed for a Cree audience. Campbell and Wheeler argue that only those who know the language and culture could determine the status of certain characters based on actual people or recognize the references to sacred Cree stories. Likewise, it is only the Cree reader who can decipher Ahenakew's embedded codes or recognize *word bundles*. Wheeler summarizes Campbell's argument:

> In the stories of Chief Thunderchild and Old Keyam, [Campbell] explains, are the teachings of napewatsowin, man ways,[22] in the context of nêhiyawêwin, Cree ways. Encoded for future generations are instructions on how to be warriors, providers, and protectors in an ever changing world.[23]

I am persuaded by Campbell and Wheeler that the text is full of word bundles, teaching nêhiyawêwin. I build on their insights to interrogate the contradiction in *Voices of the Plains Cree*, with excerpts that defend Cree and Métis nêhiyawi-itâpisinowin, of worldviews juxtaposed with more vitriolic passages that seem to be critical of the Cree and more allied with the colonizer's agenda. I query to what extent a demonstration of respect for different perspectives and a tolerance for differing points of view is part of a Cree worldview.

But there is an added complexity. In 2005, while a graduate student, I relied on *Voices of the Plains Cree*, edited in 1973 by Ruth M. Buck, to study Ahenakew. In my analysis of his writing, I struggled with harsh critical points about Cree practices, values, and ideas, that were embedded in his more generous storytelling. Little did I know that a decade later I would be able to access hundreds of handwritten pages of his work, stored in the Province of Saskatchewan archives. Little could I have imagined that I would then have the much-needed aid of Research Assistants to transcribe Ahenakew's cursive into searchable word documents.[24] It is only now, when I can compare Ahenakew's original, unpublished manuscript, *Old Keyam*, with *Voices of the Plains* Cree, that I can determine the extent of Buck's edits, including her outright changes to Ahenakew's words. I have come to realize that some of the harshest contradictions in the published version are not actually present in the original, unpublished *Old Keyam* manuscript.

For example, from his life story, we know that Ahenakew was terribly affected by the loss of life on reserves in Saskatchewan due to the 1918 Spanish Flu epidemic. This was one of the motivating factors that had him enrol in medical school in 1920. It would not be surprising should Ahenakew include strong opinions that advocated for better access to doctors and higher medical standards. Still, in Buck's 1973 version, Ahenakew purportedly wrote:

> The settled life imposed upon the Indian demands a complete change of habits. He has exchanged the teepee for a shanty of logs, mud-chinked, badly ventilated, poorly lighted, and over-crowded. He has lost his freedom to roam, and never thinks to remove the refuse that collects about his dwelling. Over-crowded conditions discourage any cleanliness; ignorance contributes to his children's malnourishment. The old life developed gregarious customs. Now on reserves, two or three families will often crowd into a dwelling not large enough for one family, sleeping and eating in the same room, keeping the door and the windows shut against the cold. When constant danger menaced us from every side we accepted the uncertainty of life with a stoic fatalism that carries over now into our disregard for the simplest rules of health. I have seen a consumptive person dying on a shake-down on the floor, the can into which he spat emptied just outside the door, and flies swarming everywhere.[25]

The image of ignorance is jarring, with the Indian living in substandard housing, surrounded by garbage, without the knowledge to properly nourish children of the household; the cultural value of hospitality has convinced Indigenous people to live too close to one another, jeopardizing their health; the cultural value of stoicism causes them to disregard basic rules of hygiene.

With Buck's edits, as we shall see, the narrative effectively blames the Indigenous person; meanwhile Ahenakew had a different goal. In the manuscript, before Buck edited it, Ahenakew tries to explain the factors that conspire against Indigenous people, as a way to provide critique that will improve conditions. In the unpublished *Old Keyam* manuscript Ahenakew writes:

> His settled life demanded of him a complete change of habits. Instead of the teepee, he had a little shanty of log and mud, badly ventilated and as badly lighted. He could not move this from place to place and he did not think of doing that which he never had to do before—remove the refuse from his premises. Moreover, the smallness and the over-crowded condition of the shanty, soon discouraged his wife from trying to keep it clean. When the buffalo disappeared from the prairie for ever, the struggle for existence became acute and under-nourishment was the result. Tuberculosis found in him a fertile soil.

While Buck phrases it so that the Indian "exchanges" the teepee for the shack, as though this was a voluntary move, Ahenakew simply reports that there has been a change. While Buck lists the garbage surrounding the shanty, she emphasizes that the Indian "never thinks to remove the refuse"; by comparison, Ahenakew emphasizes the changed context now necessitates a task that was never required before. Then Buck blames "over-crowded conditions" as the reason for the lack of hygiene and "ignorance" as the reason for malnourishment; by contrast, Ahenakew refers to the psychic burden of the squalor upon the wife that discourages her, referencing the near-extermination of their food source as the reason for persistent hunger, all setting the stage for disease. There seems little reason for Buck, as editor, to make the changes she has other than to put the blame for inadequate shelter and diet, and then subsequent disease, squarely on the shoulders of Indigenous people.

In the next paragraph in the unpublished manuscript, Ahenakew writes:

> The Indians had always lived together for mutual protection against the enemy; this had bred in them a gregariousness which now proved unfortunate. Two or even three families were commonly to be found in a shack not large enough for one. This condition rendered the trouble still more serious.

This paragraph is relatively similar to Buck's version. However, Buck has left out the following paragraph in which Ahenakew expresses empathy:

> Everything seemed to conspire against the health of the once strong nation. They grew weaker and less able to fight and resist disease. It persists up to the present day.

At the end of Buck version, she emphasizes that it is stoic fatalism that is to be blamed for the disregard of hygiene rules. This is not what Ahenakew wrote in the original. Instead, he laments the lack of science education. Ahenakew states:

> The Indians are ignorant of the laws of health. They do not believe in germs; does not know they exist. I have seen a consumptive dying on a shakedown made on the floor. The flies would be swarming. He may use a can into which he expectorates, and which most likely will be emptied just outside the house, there being seldom a special place provided for refuse. A whole family may sleep and eat in the same room; furthermore, if the weather is not too hot, the doors and windows may be religiously closed.

The image Ahenakew draws is concerning, especially given the contagious nature of many illnesses, particularly tuberculosis, and the ways in which flies can carry some diseases. The can is a potential spittoon, but without the guidelines to ensure it doesn't contaminate the others in the house. Ahenakew draws an image of a family in need of health education. However, in Buck's version she paints a tableau of the simple disregard for the rules of hygiene, as though there is nothing that can be done.

In Ahenakew's unpublished manuscript, he expresses a lot of criticism of health conditions, and the need for improvement. It is notable that Buck edits out much of this. For example, in the unpublished manuscript, Ahenakew uses the voice of Old Keyam to discuss residential schools—what he refers to as Boarding Schools—in Chapter 14, and relays that the three he knows well are not the worst of their kind and

> perhaps better in many ways. At least they were representative. I do not in any way question the efficiency of those who were placed over them, in fact I would rather say they needed commendation in all three cases.[26]

When you read the harrowing story he then tells about the deaths of children at these schools, it seems obvious that his careful wording is hiding critique. Buck, instead, edits Ahenakew's words to be a ringing endorsement so that Buck's published version states:

> During the years when I worked, I came to know three boarding schools. These were no worse than their kind. I think they may have been better, for those in charge knew the Indians and they did their best.[27]

In the unpublished manuscript Ahenakew then describes the large dormitories that the children sleep in, and declares that:

> what I objected to was the herding of the well with the diseased. I have seen, in these schools at times scrofulous children and consumptive children in the same sleeping room with numbers of others. I have seen them use the same towel and basins. I have never seen an effort made to supply the sick with their own cups, saucers and plates. The chance for infection is not lessened as it should be and considering the usual conditions of limited accommodation and money, it is indeed difficult to take stringent precautions – The matter seems easier to plan than to carry out.

In this case, the lack of health education lies with the schools and the result is deadly. Ahenakew continues:

> The natural consequence is not difficult to see. The rooms in time, are saturated with germs, tuberculosis finds a foothold in the school and the result is what has made these schools a source of fear to Indians in general.

All of the above-detailed critique is eliminated by Buck in the published version. Instead, Buck inserts a paragraph that is not in the original. To be clear, based on the documents that I have, I cannot determine where the following passage comes from, but it is not in the original manuscript, nor is it in the hundreds of papers to which I have access. This means that Buck inserted a piece of writing by Ahenakew from a different source, or she composed this paragraph herself. Regardless, it is an addition that disrupts the argument that Ahenakew has penned. Buck's insert is as follows:

> Now in a primitive society life expectancy can never be high; but the white man brought to us many diseases that have made us seem a dying race. Tuberculosis is everywhere amongst us, and in the past smallpox epidemics raged. These the white man dreads too, and has learned largely to control. There are others that he may regard less seriously—take even measles for instance, to which he is relatively immune. Any of these can be deadly to us, and particularly to our children.[28]

Then Buck leaves out the specific points of concern that Ahenakew has articulated in his unpublished manuscript about the natural consequences of the negligence of hygiene standards that he witnessed in residential schools. Given these hygiene standards are *largely known*, Buck's reference to low life expectancy in *primitive* society and illnesses that *the white man dreads too*, seems to be a strategy to mitigate the criticism that residential schools could have prevented disease and death.

Buck also makes small modifications to Ahenakew's writing. For example, in the unpublished manuscript Ahenakew pens the following:

> The life of strict barrack discipline, the thwarting of the most natural instincts of the Indian child, the close confinement, the different food, the lack of outdoor life to which he has been accustomed for hundreds of generations all serve to lower his vitality and make him susceptible to the germs which he is breathing in every night.

Buck includes this passage exactly as Ahenakew has written it, except for the last phrase. Where Ahenakew states that "the Indian child" is susceptible "to the germs which he is breathing in every night," Buck changes this to say instead that these circumstances "make him *still* more susceptible, certainly to tuberculosis" (emphasis mine). It is the addition of *still* that reorients the sentence, that distracts the reader from the unhygienic conditions of the school—something she does not mention—and instead suggests that the children are at risk but come to the school with health issues. This is directly opposite to Ahenakew's original, unpublished text when he writes:

> Is it a wonder that there is such a high percentage of deaths from tuberculosis in these schools! From our reserve there went, a great many children, healthy ones, boys and girls, to a certain Boarding School. Today not a single one of those is alive. The school was good in every way other than this, that it was saturated with germs.

In the unpublished version Ahenakew makes clear that the problem is with the sanitation standards of the school, a point that Buck edits out. At the end of this monologue in the unpublished manuscript, the character of Old Keyam asks the following:

> I ask any sane man, would it not have been better if these children had stayed home rather than to go to that school? I have seen again and again children come home from these schools in the last stages of consumption – come home to die after having lost the natural joy of association with their parents, brothers and sisters, victims of a well-meant but not over wise Educational policy. I am not here speaking of the silent heartache of the stoic fathers nor the child-like moaning sobs of the poor helpless Indian mother unheard by the world. I use not these to prove my contention.[29]

Buck includes almost the same passage in *Voices of the Plains Cree* except for the first sentence, the question addressed to the sane man; she also eliminates the description of the parents. She simply states: "Their parents' sense of loss, and their grief, I need not dwell upon here, nor use it to support my contention."[30] There is a depersonalization of the narrative that truncates its rhetorical power.

This deformation of the manuscript is not reflected in how Buck portrayed her influence as an editor to potential publishers. In a letter dated 28 January 1969 to Dr. Ahab Spence,[31] the Head of Cultural Development, in the Department of Indian Affairs and Northern Development, Buck declares her editing philosophy. She states:

> These fourteen chapters have in fact been rewritten from the original twenty-five given in the outline of the first manuscript. Most of the original material is in rough form, the first draft only, with corrections and cancellations. Some chapters are missing. I have been most scrupulous in my re-writing to use only the material from Edward Ahenakew's own manuscript, including some short articles that are listed in the index as Item III.[32] (underlined in the original)

From a comparison of Ahenakew's original with Buck's version, however, it is clear that Buck was less scrupulous than she states.

For another example, in Buck's published version, Keyam defends the Sun Dance and other Cree religious practices, asking, "Why should individuals be forced to give up what they consider to be a means of reconciliation with the author of their being?"[33] Yet earlier in Buck's text, Old Keyam defends the "prohibition by Canadian law" of the mâhtâhitowin (the give-away dance),[34] "for it is like a drunken orgy, releasing all that is most reckless in Indians."[35] The effect of declarations made confidently in one place and retracted in another gives the "Old Keyam" text an unstable feeling.

This is even more unstable and confusing when it becomes obvious that nowhere in the unpublished *Old Keyam* manuscript originally conceived of by Ahenakew is there a discussion of the Sun Dance or a discussion of prohibitions of Canadian law. In fact, there are few references to dance at all. In Chapter One, "Old Keyam, an 'Old Man' of the Band," there is a rather innocuous criticism by Old Keyam that "the religious Indian dances did not have much moral effect.... no really elevating effect."[36] Besides which, Old Keyam reports, in the middle of the unpublished chapter four, titled "A Prairie Indian Reserve":

> They tell me, too, that the Indian dances are now a thing of the past, the white man's way of gliding around with a woman to the notes of some musical instrument having been adopted. The sick are never conjured over, for the more pretentious white-man doctor now gives his pills and bottles to the ailing.[37]

Yet in the unpublished manuscript, after he makes these statements in Chapter Four, and he contemplates how uneasy he is about the ways in which Cree customs have been disrupted on this successful reserve, he almost immediately expresses remorse about speaking too plainly. In the original, unpublished version Ahenakew says nothing more about dance.

Instead, Ahenakew discusses dancing in a collection titled "nonhuman personalities" that is completely separate from the *Old Keyam* manuscript. Here he writes in the first person about how he has learned about wîhtikow (weetigo, the Cannibal Spirit), mêmêkwêsiwak (the Little Folk), and pâhkahkos (the Hard-Luck Spirit featured in the Give-Away Dance). Ahenakew warns the reader that he hasn't been able to corroborate what he has learned about the pâhkahkos, the bony spectre, a Hunger Spirit, a spirit being,[38] an indication that this story is not meant to be taken as documented research, as some of his writing for anthropological venues have been, but for the pleasure of listening. And Ahenakew sets a spooky scene.

Ahenakew describes his travels with Sam Cook through "scenery [that] was so primeval it was almost weird." Sam plays the role of cultural guide and identifies where he and Frank Laducere had previously heard the cackle of the pâhkahkos who then, without wings, flies off. Then he takes Ahenakew in the direction the pâhkahkos had flown. Here are portions of the rest of Ahenakew's story:

> I have seen the dance which is made in his [pâhkahkos'] honor. It is called mah-tah-e-to-win [mâhtâhitowin]. The white people call it the give-away-dance – by the way it is prohibited by the Canadian laws because it is said to be impoverizing.

Ahenakew later explains that:

> The giving away of things such as horses, harness, bedding, clothing and lesser things is done to the honor of pâhkahkos, the Spirit who gives food so lavishly to those whom he favors.
>
> I have seen many Indian dances but never have I seen one which seems to call out what is most reckless in Indians. It was like a drunken orgy.

A friend of mine, as a rule a very quiet friendly fellow came near me and I still, after the lapse of three decades, can see that wild look in his eyes—[For the moment I felt I hated him]. He had given away his team wagon and clothing to people who, because of improvidence, had nothing of any value to give him in return. Thus ends my own experience.

This is just a fragment of Ahenakew as a storyteller at his finest. He sets the scene, hints at how unsettled and uneasy he and his travelling companion were feeling, and then introduces the dance, to give a sense of the frenzy this dance was causing, describing the confusing rituals as he is introduced to each part.

What is remarkable when comparing Ahenakew's story with the version edited by Buck and published in *Voices of the Plains Cree* is the extent to which his completely polished story is changed. To start, in Buck's version Ahenakew had been told a pâhkahkos story by Cook but she changes the narrative so that Ahenakew is travelling alone, with no anxiety when greeting the host. Second, in Ahenakew's version, the delight exists in not understanding everything.[39] In comparison, Buck has very little tolerance for uncertainty; for her every part of the story needs to be explicated in detail. In the unpublished text, Ahenakew shares some of the mystery and thrill of a rarely seen dance, and concludes by saying:

Whether these two beings [mêmêkwêsiwak and pâhkahkos] ever existed actually, I cannot say, but I would not like to see the idea of them as it is in the Indian mind even in these days fade away into the mists of oblivion and the land through which they may have prowled know them no more.[40]

However, Buck's version opposes Ahenakew's wish that these beings be remembered; she concludes this passage with a judgement: "I knew then why the dance is prohibited by Canadian law, for it is like a drunken orgy, releasing all that is most reckless in Indians."[41]

Buck takes this story by Ahenakew, which was not in the unpublished *Old Keyam* in the first place, inserts it into the *Voices of the Plains Cree*, makes arbitrary choices that diminish the suspense, and uses the story to justify the outlawing of a dance that Ahenakew wants to persist.

It is remarkable that as an Anglican minister, Ahenakew is so tolerant of Cree lifeways, especially given Buck's intolerance. I suggest that Cree-Métis philosopher Lorraine Brundige's articulation of the cultural value of kihcêyihtamowin, respect between people,[42] is evident. Ahenakew exhibits the ability to tolerate different points of view in order to value and preserve respectful relationships.

Within his narrative Ahenakew demonstrates how opposition might be overlooked in deference to kihcêyihtamowin. When Old Keyam is newly married to Chochena, they travel to a conference on Indian education where he participates as an interpreter. Keyam mentions that he and his wife have discussed the speeches given there many times—pleased that she is keen to attend and that she can repeat almost everything that was said during the sessions. It is from this position of respect that he states that Chochena "heartily agrees with that Western Chief who advocated each reserve paying so much a year to help the financing of schools. In point of fact she has almost converted me to that view."[43]

Keyam admits that though this Chief's motion was defeated, he "certainly showed up well."[44] Keyam, however, is convinced by another: "The Chief from Carlton way, who opposed him was one of the best too. His manly deportment, and natural force attracted and commanded the respect of all."[45]

Rather than discredit Chochena or other people with opposing opinions, Keyam practices kihcêyihtamowin. While he signals the importance of debate as he relates the content of different arguments, he takes care to articulate his respect for all participants.

Keyam understands that the Cree value of kihcêyihtamowin, "respect between people," comes out of a complex epistemological system based on the interrelationship of all things, wâhkôhtowin. Rather than the famous Cartesian mind/body split or the hierarchies of human beings over animals and plants, the animate over the inanimate, Cree philosophy is based on the concept that everything is interconnected, and kihcêyihtamowin is the respectful recognition of these relationships. As Lorraine Brundige states, "Far more important than having the same beliefs was an ability to engage in respectful interaction."[46]

Ahenakew's nephew Stan Cuthand writes a 1978 article about his uncle that suggests that, in Cuthand's view, Ahenakew was not so much respectful as acquiescent to dominant powers. He states that while Ahenakew "worked hard with the League of Indians," he was "not aggressive in his approach to rectify the wrongs of his people, he was caught between two worlds, and was often more loyal to the church."[47] While I can understand why Cuthand, as a member of a younger generation than Ahenakew's, would be impatient with Ahenakew's seemingly subservient ways, I suggest that Ahenakew is more complicated than Cuthand suggests; that Ahenakew was both a British loyalist and an insightful government critic, both a devoted Christian clergyman and a proud Cree at the same time. Every way he turned, whether to his community or his congregation, the message he wanted to share was respect.

Brundige confirms the role of respect in Cree culture.[48] She quotes Abel Chapman, a Cree elder: "A long time ago the youngsters gathered around an elder, like we sit around the TV today. The elder would relate stories about survival. That's how the children learned."[49] This is not to suggest that Cree learners complacently accepted the words of authority. Brundige argues that embedded in Cree philosophy was the capacity to hold conflicting points of view, noting that the value of maintaining good relations was more important than epistemological differences.[50] Brundige argues that because of the belief in multiple perspectives, perceptual differences were accommodated in traditional society: "Historically, Swampy Cree people were prepared to accept 'other' stories and found no contradiction in the idea that Europeans and Swampy Crees had different beliefs about the world."[51]

In Cree epistemology, respectful interaction functions as a core value.[52]

In "Remembering the Poetics of Ancient Sound kistêsinâw/wîsahkêcâhk's maskihkiy (Elder Brother's Medicine)," Tasha Beeds describes Edward Ahenakew:

> As a nêhiyaw nâpêw, an Anglican minister, a writer, a language speaker, and a leader of the people, Ahenakew was an okihcihtâw (a worthy young man/provider) of his era. He drew upon the traditions of the Old Ones within the nexus of Christianity, showing how nêhiyaw culture is living and dynamic. In creating multiple dialogues between our world and English, Ahenakew created new discursive possibilities that we are still learning from.[53]

In a time of tremendous change and challenges, Ahenakew tried, as an expression of a Cree value, to make peace with the viewpoints of both the Cree and of the colonizers, by trying to hold what sometimes were irreconcilable perspectives.

His tolerance for different perspectives is well documented in an early notebook that exists in the Province of Saskatchewan archives that begins before 1912 and ends around 1915, a notebook that to date has never been published.[54] At the end of this notebook, Ahenakew writes about Indian mysticism and beliefs, as something just as legitimate as western ideas. Near the end of this unpublished entry, Ahenakew writes that:

> I have personally heard some intelligent white men, who had been conversant with Indian life in days gone by, tell of things they have seen some Indians do, that they could not account for as squaring up with any known natural laws.... I myself believed such things when a child. After receiving a little education, I in foolish cocky mood, declared that since it (as I supposed) clashed with learning,

it was all rot.[55] I have received a little more education since, have seen a little more of life, and I today am where I was when a child. I believe, and I believe now, not altogether blindly, but considering the belief of the Indian, considering the neglect of studies like Psychology among the whites, and their social characteristics against any healthy subjective knowledge of such subjects, considering the belief of some in such minor things, like Hypnotism, Mesmerism, Spiritualism, considering the boundless superiority of Mind over Matter, considering a hundred other things, the cumulative value of all these gives the subject at least a degree of possibility and a faint touch of probability which ought to command at least a little bit of respect and attention from the thinking world.[56]

It is in this attitude of respect for the beliefs of his people, and his ability to tolerate conflicting ideas and perspectives, where Ahenakew demonstrates his value of kihcêyihtamowin, a value that underlies his work.

*âskaw, kîspin kîkway kinôhtê-kiskêyihtên, ohcitaw piko
ta-pêhoyan isko naskwêwasihowin takopayiki.
pawâtamowinihk ta-kî-takopayinwa naskwêwasihowina.*

*Sometimes, if you need to know something, you have
to wait until the answer comes to you.
Answers can come in dreams.*

CHAPTER FOUR

Edward Ahenakew's Intertwined Unpublished Life-Inspired Stories

âniskwâcimopicikêwin in *Old Keyam* and *Black Hawk*

Cree intellectual and Anglican cleric Edward Ahenakew was born in 1885— the year it all went wrong—the year of the North West Rebellion, the year Métis hero Louis Riel was hanged, the year Ahenakew's great-uncle, the Cree Chief Poundmaker, among others, was sent to prison. Ahenakew was born on the Ah-tah-ka-koops Reserve, now known as Ahtahkakoop First Nation, as part of a large Cree-speaking family, the son of one of several Ahenakew brothers, several with lifelong affiliations with the Anglican church. He attended day school in his home community of Sandy Lake until the age of eleven; between 1896 and 1903, he went to residential school in Prince Albert, Saskatchewan; in 1905, he travelled to Toronto to study theology; after he completed his studies in Saskatchewan in 1912, he was ordained as an Anglican priest.[1] Cree journalist Doug Cuthand called Edward Ahenakew "an unsung hero"[2] and "Our Martin Luther King," because he was a devoted leader for nêhiyawak.

Yet Ahenakew was also a writer, even though his fiction and much of his creative non-fiction were never published during his lifetime. After his passing in 1961, his niece Katherine Greyeyes saved his boxes of tattered, mostly hand-written papers and gave them to trusted family friend Ruth Matheson Buck, the daughter of an Anglican priest that Ahenakew had served with. Buck edited two of Ahenakew's works—the stories of Chief Thunderchild and a semi-autobiographical work called *Old Keyam*—and bundled them together for publication as *Voices of the Plains Cree* (1973). She then deposited Ahenakew's papers into the Saskatchewan provincial archives, where they are available for researchers to consult. For whatever reason, Buck took no interest in Ahenakew's other papers, neglecting significant contributions such as his nearly completed novel, *Black Hawk*, despite the fact that she could have brought to the attention of the public the first novel written by an Indigenous author in Canada.[3]

Part of the work that my research team has done is to transcribe Ahenakew's work from the cursive, making it easier to read and to search.[4] In this chapter, I discuss the ending of Ahenakew's last three handwritten chapters of the unpublished autobiographical manuscript, *Old Keyam*, completed in the early 1920s, that Buck decided not to include in her version, as part of *Voices of the Plains Cree*, and compare these chapters with Ahenakew's unpublished novel, *Black Hawk*, full of autobiographical clues, written circa 1918.

My principal argument is that it is impossible to understand Ahenakew without access to all his work, including the portions of his writing that Buck edited out of what she published, as well as the rest of his remaining unpublished papers. Without access to all of the Ahenakew corpus, it is difficult to identify the interconnectedness of his work, what Neal McLeod has called âniskwâcimopicikêwin, translated as "the process of connecting stories together."[5] McLeod chooses this term rather than "intertextuality, which often presupposes an 'oral-written' binary." In other words, McLeod discusses the ways that stories affect our understanding of other stories that exist in a similar circuit. McLeod includes not just writing but also oral narratives from the "land, dreams, petroglyphs, classical narratives, hide paintings, and so on."[6]

It is clear that Ahenakew is allied to the written word in both English and Cree, as well as to questions in the Cree imagination. For example, works such as *Black Hawk* and *Old Keyam* are clearly inspired by epistolary fiction, and include an assembly of documents, letters, reports. Both also include a range of discourses that might be marked as oral in nature such as sermons, speeches, reported conversation, recorded story. Regardless of the method of the delivery of the stories, whether written or oral, Ahenakew's work cites different narratives from different perspectives that prioritizes a vision of Cree history. Because of this, his corpus can only be understood by reading his stories alongside each other, as an example of âniskwâcimopicikêwin.

Ahenakew's earliest writing is a notebook written around 1910, when he would have been in his mid-twenties. This notebook contains poetry written among grocery lists, notes about Christmas and the occasional doodle, alongside musings on the Mind, Will, Psychology. His notebook conveys his struggle as a young man to connect his responsibilities as a Cree and a Christian given the context, with a great deal of cultural loss due to colonialism; it is not surprising that he expresses ambivalence. For example, one of the first poems in Ahenakew's earliest notebook is about a dream he had about an ancestor that comes to him in a vision and says to him:

I am thy father far removed
Long centuries intervene
Between the Time that now is yours
And last, that I was seen.

I hovered o'er thy troubled mind
And saw it go astray
You have espoused the whiteman's Christ
And led our youth astray.

This unpublished poem, written in youth, gives a hint of his personal struggles with the adoption of Christianity by nêhiyaw people; the poem sits in opposition to the sermons and church material written by Ahenakew and published during his lifetime. The fact that Ahenakew discusses this as a dream is significant as dreams in a Cree context are to be taken seriously as primary sources of knowledge and a recognized way that ancestors, or knowledge authorities, might connect with us. Here Ahenakew is emphasizing the gravity of cultural change by having a "father far removed," an ancestor, question his conversion to Christianity and his chosen profession as an evangelist.

This does not alter the fact that Ahenakew had a life-long career as a committed cleric, dedicated to Cree people. He was also hungry for more education and, after witnessing the devastating loss of life due to the Spanish flu in 1918–19, Ahenakew enrolled in medical school at the University of Alberta.

In the 1921 edition of *Evergreen and Gold*, the yearbook distributed by the University of Alberta, there are entries devoted to the prospective doctors who were scheduled to graduate as part of the class of 24. The entry devoted to Ahenakew describes him as a writer:

> "Now boys don't excite yourselves: there's another day for Anatomy."
> "Hen" has wide interests outside Varsity, as head of the Saskatchewan Branch of the Canadian League of Indians, and a writer of no mean ability. This class congratulates itself on possessing such a representative of the original Canadians.

While this particular entry includes a quote by Ahenakew himself, most of the entries for the other students do not begin in this same way, indicating that the yearbook editors thought this quote captured his voice in a way that would be recognizable to his classmates. Whether the words of the quote were said with enthusiasm or sarcasm, this entry creates an image of Ahenakew as a welcome and accomplished peer.

Ahenakew is also recorded in the personal papers of historian Paul A. W. Wallace, who met Ahenakew as part of the University of Alberta's writing club. Wallace's diaries record the fact that they regularly discussed writing and that Ahenakew was frustrated by the lack of opportunity to publish. On Sept 19, 1924, Wallace described Ahenakew's meeting with Dr. Lorne Pierce, editor of Ryerson Press: "[Ahenakew] was so disgusted with Dr. Pierce's inability to talk business that he very nearly broke off the arrangement."[7] At this point in time, Ahenakew's *Old Keyam* manuscript had been in the hands of Pierce for at least two years and ultimately was never published during his lifetime.

It was during the period from his ordination in 1912 up until 1925, from his late twenties and all through his thirties, that Ahenakew was his most creative. During these years, he wrote at least three short stories, influenced by romance, with an ear to comedy; the novel, *Black Hawk*, about an earnest, devout young Cree minister in medical school struggling with his love for a white woman; and a semi-autobiographical rumination of the future of Indigenous people called *Old Keyam*. Ahenakew aspired for all of these to be published. And most of them were not.

By the early twenties (1922–23), Ahenakew was forced to give up his studies because of a breakdown in his health. His convalescence took him to the Onion Lake Reserve where, once he gained his strength, he began interviewing the elderly Chief Thunderchild, also known as kâ-pitikow, who had been a follower of Big Bear. Ahenakew took brief notes as he listened to the stories.[8] As mentioned previously, Buck included these interviews in the first half of *Voices of the Plains Cree*.

By 1925, the year he turned 40, and then for the second half of his life, Ahenakew continued to write, although much of it was part of his position as a minister or cultural expert. It was then, in 1925, that he began writing a Church publication called the *Cree Monthly Guide*, bilingual in Cree and English, that he produced on a mimeograph machine as part of his duties as a Minister. It was in his forties that he submitted âtayôhkêwina—a genre of sacred stories about wîsahkêcâhk (also spelled in various forms including Wesageechak), the Cree Trickster—to *The Journal of American Folklore*, published in 1929.[9] He wrote church histories, school histories, family genealogies, church sermons, letters. He contributed to a Cree dictionary. He still occasionally tried to find publication for his creative work, but to no success.

In this chapter, I examine the most suggestive incidents of autobiography that exist in Edward Ahenakew's unpublished work, including the unedited "semi-autobiographical" manuscript version of *Old Keyam*[10] and his autobiographical novel *Black Hawk*.[11] What is fascinating is that the two unpublished manuscripts seem to have a character in common, both referred to as

Young Hawk, although in *Old Keyam* he is also referred to as Eli and in *Black Hawk* the hero's first name is Allan. When editor Ruth M. Buck edited and condensed some of Ahenakew's papers for publication, including *Old Keyam*, in what she titled *Voices of the Plains Cree*, released in 1973, she omitted his final scene with Keyam on his deathbed: in these omitted scenes, Keyam passes on his pipe to a new character named Young Hawk, who struggles because of his love for a white woman.[12]

The dilemma of a cross-racial romance is also featured in the unpublished novel, *Black Hawk*, as two heroes from two different generations struggle with love. The first Black Hawk leaves Cree territory in the 1880s, in what is now Saskatchewan, and travels with some Hudson Bay men to Ottawa, only to fall in love with a white woman whom he can never marry; he returns home and subsequently dies in battle against the Blackfoot. *Black Hawk* also features a second hero born a generation later, Black Hawk's nephew, named Allan Hawk, who likewise falls in love with a young white woman, Helen.[13]

In two autobiographical essays, "The Story of Rev. Canon Edward Ahenakew" and "Genealogical Sketch of my Family," Ahenakew describes his uncle Na-pas-kis, who is clearly the model for *Black Hawk*. Na-pas-kis, like the first Black Hawk in the novel, goes back east on an adventure and returns home a changed person; eventually, he volunteers to fight the Blackfoot and is killed in battle. Ahenakew was a lifelong bachelor, and no evidence suggests that he had suffered a failed romance. Regardless, this theme fascinated him. The problem of having to choose between one's vocation and a beloved is a tension in *Black Hawk*, a tension that is replicated in Ahenakew's devotion to his Church and his commitment to his Cree community. Yet while the romance genre typically is filled with tension between the hero and heroine, and ends with a clear resolution, in *Black Hawk*, the tension is not quickly or clearly resolved.

Black Hawk, written circa 1918, opens with a storyteller named Owl telling an audience of children about their "grandfather's younger brother,"[14] Black Hawk. Owl describes this handsome and well-loved uncle, respected by both "Indian" and whites, who twice travelled to Ottawa and "returned a great man."[15] Although he was the youngest of five capable brothers, "because of the favour shown to him by whites and Indians and the love and pride of his brothers with regard to him, he would have been made Chief."[16]

Upon Black Hawk's last return from Ottawa, his sisters-in-law and brothers "noted in his demeanour a preoccupied air." Black Hawk admits to his oldest brother:

> "There is trouble that weighs heavy in my heart, my manhood is put to much strain. Two thousand miles is a long way brother," He took

a picture out of his pocket and handed it over. His brother looked at it and it proved to be a picture of a girl, a white girl with smiling eyes. "In Ottawa, her horse ran away and I stopped the horse. She was good to me because I saved her life. She gave me her likeness and I came away. My brother will be the only one that will know."

The older man sat silently and then handed back the picture. "Twenty hundreds of miles is far, my brother but that is no obstacle. Something else is more difficult than the distance. You are no fool—you know what I mean.[17]

Early in the novel, therefore, Ahenakew uses the story of doomed love, separated by a racial divide, to make clear that even the most heroic, respected, admired, well-travelled Indigenous protagonist, cannot cross the colour line.

Black Hawk, also called Napasees,[18] decides to distract himself with acts of bravery and sets off with nine other warriors to raid the Blackfoot, only to be killed in battle with the rest. When the Blackfoot Chief discovers on Black Hawk's body important papers from Ottawa along with the picture of the girl, he instructs that Black Hawk is to be buried without his body being violated.

All of this resonates with Ahenakew's stories of his grandfather's youngest brother Napaskis, as described in "Genealogical Sketch of my Family":

A white man of importance took to this handsome youth. He liked him so much that he invited him to join his party when he went back to Montreal. Napaskis went with him gladly of course. He was away for a whole year; how he spent his time there, we do not know. Enough it is to say that when he did get back, he seemed to be different. He was no longer the light-hearted young man who enjoyed the ordinary everyday life of an Indian. Something seemed to prey on his mind; he was restless.

After distributing presents among his sisters-in-law he told his brothers that he was going to Blackfeet country with the view of bringing away some of their horses. They, of course would not stop him, though they tried to dissuade him from going away so soon after his arrival.[19]

Napaskis perishes in battle and Ahenakew comments:

The sisters-in-law of Napaskis had always been very fond of him. The question they asked each other was "Why did he seem so restless and preoccupied? Why did he rush off to fight the enemy?" They wondered if Napaskis had fallen in love with some white woman down East, had found her love to be hopeless? Woman-like, they allowed their imaginations to run riot.[20]

Ahenakew then mentions that his uncle Kakasoo went to the Blackfoot reserve in 1906 and uncovered the Blackfoot version of the story, in which papers were found on Napaskis's body from the white man whom he accompanied to Montreal and, upon the advice of the Roman Catholic priest, the Blackfoot decided to bury Napaskis and the papers together, rather than follow the custom of desecrating the body of a fallen enemy.[21] Both stories—in the novel and in Ahenakew's genealogy—mirror each other, although the fictional version contains more detailed speculation about what it was that troubled the young hero.

After the story of the first Black Hawk, the novel turns to the life of Black Hawk's nephew, also called Black Hawk until he is an adult, when he is referred to as "Allan Hawk" or "Young Hawk." It is not difficult to link the biographical details of this young protagonist to details in Edward Ahenakew's life. Both were so ill as young boys that their mothers followed the model of the bible story of Samuel, offering their children to the priesthood should their lives be spared.[22] Both the fictitious Allan Hawk and Edward Ahenakew were excellent students. Both the fictitious Allan Hawk and Edward Ahenakew gave popular sermons in Saskatoon.

About halfway through the novel, Allan Hawk gives a sermon that afterwards is described by the omniscient narrator: "In every gesture was an eloquence, his words were given with ease, dignity, and superb oratory which had always been characteristic of his race."[23] His sermon fills almost five pages:

> My subject for this morning deals with the Education of our young and I would say that in my opinion therein lies the key that will open the door wherein is locked the secret which long experience in Indian Affairs has failed to solve, after 40 or 50 years of work, secular + [sic] religious.[24]

This is the topic of the sermon that Edward Ahenakew gave in 1918 in the Diocesan Women's Auxiliary (called the W.A.) and Deanery meetings, as reported on page six of the June 1, 1918 edition of the *Saskatoon Daily Star.* The headline reads: "Kindly, Yet Severe Criticism of Treatment of Indians is Voiced by Native Clergyman."[25] The smaller headline reads: "Rev. Edward Ahenakew, of Saskatchewan Diocese, Speaks of His People as One Who Knows—Says All Indian Needs is Chance to Be Educated—More Schools Needed."

And the comparison between the life of Edward Ahenakew and the fictional Allan Hawk continues. Both studied medicine, although Ahenakew had to quit his studies due to ill health, while the novel ends before we know whether Allan Hawk attains his degree.[26]

In fact, the ending of the novel is inconclusive. In the novel, Allan Hawk—like his uncle before him—falls in love with a white girl; yet while his uncle faced unarticulated obstacles, there appears to be less resistance to the love story in the next generation. Allan Hawk is so exceptional, so talented, so upstanding, that the family of his love interest, Helen, uniformly embrace him, from Helen's brother-in-law Harry to her Scottish father and her sister Alice; the only racism expressed is by the beloved Helen, giving Allan Hawk the chance to reply and refute her assumptions.[27] The result is that the reader can see Allan Hawk thrive in the public sphere (mostly) free from racism and at the same time follow the feelings of Helen, who dismisses Allan Hawk at first but grows to question her racist assumptions in order to love him.

At the novel's end, Helen has moved from Saskatoon to Winnipeg to study nursing. Allan Hawk has returned from the First World War to complete his medical studies in Winnipeg and the couple meet. They rendezvous a few times on a bridge and discuss topics of varying intimacy. He affirms to her that he is "one of the few who have pledged our lives to effect [improved conditions for his people],"[28] a dramatic moment that seems to indicate that he would choose his people over her and that there is no way they can be together. Still, they meet again the next night on the same bridge and she asks him about his home. He talks about the "weird but sweet + [sic] wild call of the loons as he calls its mate and she replies,"[29] giving the reader some sense that Allan and Helen might have a future together. But in the final paragraph, Allan describes the beauty of the moon rising across the lake, with him sitting around a campfire with his parents "and the rest. I am again an Indian boy, as I used to be, carefree and home loving and I love it." Whether he is offering her the chance to join him is not clear. On the one hand, the image of the loons suggests a union; on the other, the image of the hero returning as a child to his parents suggests his community is his priority. Possible answers lie in the unpublished sections of *Old Keyam*.

Ahenakew's editor Ruth M. Buck has been recognized as Ahenakew's literary advocate. Without her labour, we would not have the considerable archive that we have today. She organized his papers and transcribed his work from the cursive, and put considerable effort into finding publishing venues for his writing. However, an examination of the originals in comparison with her edits reveals that Buck has not been completely accurate when she states, in her introduction to the 1973 edition of *Voices of the Plains Cree*, that "no material other than Edward Ahenakew's is used in the assembling of this work."[30] She gives the impression that she has preserved Ahenakew's words down to the detail, in correspondence with several administrators in the Department of Indian Affairs and Northern Development.[31] Since the funds that they administered were specifically for publishing manuscripts by Indigenous peoples, they would only be interested in Ahenakew's writing. Yet when Buck edited *Old Keyam* and released the shortened version as the second half of *Voices of the Plains Cree*, she admitted that she couldn't bring herself to include the final chapters of the unpublished manuscript. In her typed notes on her progress working on the Ahenakew papers, she states:

> I found it quite impossible to accept the final chapters [of *Old Keyam*] which were written in the sentimental style of popular novels of that time, and pulp magazines. These were about Keyam's marriage, his later death-bed scene, and the passing of his pipe to Hawk.
>
> I happened to know the story of the actual marriage upon which he based the idea of Keyam's. Old Wezo (one of Thunderchild's companions in warfare) married Georgina, an old woman whose first husband had been a noted Cree of that same time of warfare, and whose son, Johnny Saskatchewan, was a well-known guide.
>
> The two old people were Onion Lake Indians. Old Georgina was a general favorite of all our family—we called her "grandmother", and she welcomed us always into her tent.
>
> Edward Ahenakew married them a year or two after we left the Mission, but we were delighted to hear the story of Wezo's courtship—and I have drawn upon that in reconstructing the story of the marriage of Old Keyam and Chochena.
>
> The death-scene and young Hawk's dilemma in falling in love with a white-girl, I have simply washed out.[32]

Kristina Bidwell also makes reference to Buck's omissions, and concludes: "Thus, we do not have easy access to Ahenakew's writings as they were composed."[33]

When comparing the end of Ahenakew's hand-written version of *Old Keyam* with the ending that Buck supplies for *Voices of the Plains Cree*, it is clear that Buck took liberties with content and style. These changes significantly alter the ending that Ahenakew composed.

For example, in the original handwritten Chapter Twenty, titled "Management of Indian Money," Old Keyam is wrapping up a long deliberation on the financial implications of treaties, the Indian Act, and the government. Somewhat fatigued, the character, Old Keyam, states:

> Chief, I have said enough on these subjects; they are my own fanciful interpretations of the feelings of our Indians. How far my old ideas are prejudiced I do not know. I may misjudge the minds and

feelings of the rising generation. I do not know. How far the decay of my sight and faculties have led me astray, I do not know. Advise your young men to look upon my views as belonging to a passing generation, and climb higher, by doing the best that is in them to solve the Indian problem—not by talking as I do, but by working early and late, by observing how white men go about the settling of their homesteads. Tell them to get their children education, as if life depended upon it, for it does. Heaven forbid that in my last talk on our relationship with the Government, I should put wrong ideas in the minds of your men—I am old, I have not been well, and as "An Old Man" of a band, I feel my responsibility. From now on I will leave the department out of my talks and say my say on other matters.[34]

After this declaration, the handwritten original version of *Old Keyam* continues on for three more chapters: "The Death of Old Keyam," "The Mantle Falls on the Hawk," and "The End of the Trail but … "[35]

However, Buck ends *Voices of the Plains Cree* in the earlier chapter on money management. While at first glance the original passage and Buck's edited version seem to be similar, everything in bold in the following are her additions:

> Chief, I have talked enough on these **matters. I am not going to say more. It is no use. I have tried to express the feelings of us all, but [h]**ow far my old ideas are prejudiced I do not know. I may misjudge the minds and feelings of the **new** generation, **and that too** I do not know. **Nor do I know [h]**ow far the **failing** of my sight and **my other** faculties have led me astray.
>
> Advise your young men to look upon my views as **those that [belong]** to a passing generation. **Tell them to try to** climb higher **themselves** by doing the best that is in them to solve the Indian problem—not by talking as I do, but by working early and late, by observing how white men go about **the duties of the land. And t**ell them **above all,** to get their children [educat**ed**], as if life [depend**s**] upon it, for it does.[36]

Buck then follows this with a final page, most of which is not in the original. As an example, consider a few lines in Buck's version from one of the following paragraphs. It reads: "Keyam stopped, and the Chief, who had been listening intently rose to his feet. 'There are many times,' he said, 'when I wish that I knew as much as Old Keyam.'"[37] Nothing like the Chief's comment that Buck inserts exists in the original.

Likewise, at the end of the paragraph of Buck's edited version, when the Chief praises Old Keyam in front of the young men, the Chief states:

"Sometimes I think that when all the rest of us are forgotten, Old Keyam will be remembered. He thinks and says that he is old.[38] I think that Keyam lives forever."[39] This sentence is almost completely added by Buck. The phrases "he is old" and "lives forever" do not exist anywhere in the original.[40]

Also, at the end of chapter 12, in Buck's desire to craft an ending, she invents quite a bit. She invents pretty words of praise delivered by the Chief about Old Keyam. All the phrases in bold exist nowhere in the original *Old Keyam* manuscript:

> Sometimes I think that when all the rest of us are **forgotten, Old Keyam will be remembered.** He thinks and says that **he is old.** I think that Keyam **lives forever.** His words **surprised the Old Man,** and Keyam **dropped his head** to **hide his emotion.** His hands **fumbled at his belt, untying** a **leather pouch** that **glinted** with **new beads, the work of Chochena's old fingers in an old art.** "There is something here," he said, "Something that I have wanted to **show you.**"[41]

It's a charming vignette—the image of the Old Man wearing a belt crafted by his wife Chochena. Yet none of this appears in Ahenakew's version.

Similarly, much of the ending, purportedly in the words of the main character himself, is crafted by Buck:

> "**You call me** Old Keyam, and have **forgotten any other name** I might have had. I have **accepted the name** as my own. There was once a very wise man who said, '**He is wisest among you** who has found out that in truth **his wisdom** is **worth nothing** at all.'
>
> Now our **Cree language can say all that in one word,** in the name that you have given to me: *Keyam.*"

The fine words of praise that Buck writes for Old Keyam were not written by Ahenakew.

For reasons that are not explained, while Buck invents this laudatory event, she eliminates Ahenakew's ending—Ahenakew's scene at Keyam's deathbed with Keyam's wife, Chochena, crying mournfully and the band promising Keyam that they will take care of her. And Buck eliminates the scene at Old Keyam's graveside where the Chief pulls out a letter written in Cree syllabics, found in Old Keyam's smoke bag. Notice the level of literacy that Ahenakew includes in this story: the Old Chief reads the syllabics—Old Keyam's last wishes are conveyed by letter. It states,

"To Young Hawk, who has pure Indian blood in his veins and who has been to the great schools of the white man, I bequeath this red-stone pipe. He was ever thoughtful and kindly. The pipe was given to me by an old man, on his death-bed. He had said, 'As long as you own this pipe, speak words of deep thought to my children; be faithful to the trust I place in you. If you cannot fulfil the requirements of that pipe, then look you for one who is wholly Indian, one who loves his blood, and give it into his keeping with the words I have given you. Betray not the trust of Ages.

To young Hawk I pass the pipe and the words. As long as he is Indian and thinks not to mate his heart with one that is not of the tribe, he is to keep it. Otherwise the line must end; the pipe must be buried deep where no eye shall ever see it. Young Hawk, look not upon the fair ones of the other race, look to thine own, my son.

— Keyam."

Young Hawk received the pipe. The end soon came. His thoughts were with his race but his heart played him false.

When comparing the two versions, Buck's and Ahenakew's, Buck ends with Old Keyam being praised by his contemporaries, holding out "an ancient red-stone pipe-stem" and talking about the trust that was placed in him, by a previous generation. But Ahenakew emphasizes the need for the transmission of tradition by the passing of the pipe to the next generation. When Buck has the Chief state that, "Sometimes I think that when all the rest of us are forgotten, Old Keyam will be remembered," Buck is relegating Keyam's knowledge and a Cree view of the world to the past. Meanwhile Ahenakew's version includes the active passing of the pipe to Young Hawk.

Buck also eliminates the penultimate chapter, "The Mantle Falls on the Hawk," where the gift of the pipe causes Young Hawk some distress because he is in love with a young woman outside of his tribe: "Her race is white and mine is red. My Indian heart beats strong."[42] In this chapter, the voice differs from the rest of the manuscript, where it alternates between an omniscient narrator and the old man, Old Keyam's meditations; the final chapter of the unpublished *Old Keyam* is the interior monologue of Young Hawk. As he ponders his dilemma, Young Hawk thinks about the fact that even though "the day is past for Indian men," he still understands Thunder to be "piyêsiw,"[43] the Cree Thunderbird, and the Aurora Borealis to be "Ancient Men who died long ago";[44] still, this does not lift the burden of knowing that "Old Keyam has left to me the cloak I cannot wear."[45] In Young Hawk's conclusion at the end of "The Mantle Falls on the Hawk," the young hero laments the disruption of his love affair: "O Keyam, you little thought that you would be the cause of parting souls that were mated from Eternity. Your pipe, I'll keep, how long I cannot say."[46]

Ahenakew includes Hawk's realization, as a member of the next generation, that he can't live up to the standards expected in the tradition of the pipe that he was bequeathed. The final chapter, titled "The End of the Train, But—" has Young Hawk at the foot of the hill:

> beside the river, knelt young Hawk digging with a spade. In the hole he made, he placed tenderly the red stone pipe. Slowly he replaced the mud he had dug up. The line of the Old Men was ended.
> "The End of the Trail," he said to himself. "The end of that trail; but for myself and others too, there is a graded road."

Even in Hawk's struggle, he has enough respect to bury the pipe according to the instructions. And in his final sentence is the inference of hope. "'The End of the Trail,' he said to himself. 'The end of that trail; but for myself and others too, there is a graded road.'"

Buck's ending eliminates the profundity of Ahenakew's thoughts, the dilemmas Ahenakew was trying to articulate as a Cree person. Buck eliminates the struggle, the ambiguity—eliminating the very complexity that marked Ahenakew's own life as he tried to hold onto and honour some traditions while also abandoning others. And Buck's ending loses the voice of Young Hawk and his decision that the future goes forward and offers hope: "for myself and others too, there is a graded road." Even as Young Hawk abandons the responsibilities of the pipe, he understands that the paved road will take him forward. This can be interpreted in multiple ways, but only if this passage is published and read. By leaving the passage out, Buck is eliminating the discussion of an Indigenous future.

Buck's destructive editing practices mirror the practice of the publishing industry that does not recognize the importance of writings by Indigenous authors and therefore does not grant them the publishing opportunities they deserve. In Ahenakew's case it is obvious that this neglect of his writing disrupts the intertextuality or âniskwâcimopicikêwin of his work. Because the publishing world does not offer him the possibility of publication, they make an accurate understanding of his work impossible.[47]

Vexingly, there are two endings to *Old Keyam*, two final chapters titled "The End of the Trail but...," and two hand-written pages numbered 164. The first of those pages is quoted above. In the context of the *Old Keyam* manuscript, Young Hawk will not take on the persona of the Old Man to follow the title character, nor likely will anyone else. Young Hawk refuses that mantle, even though we are aware that he understands himself to be

Cree, but one born into a different time where he must take a different road. The question of the love interest is left open, because presumably with the pipe returned to the land, he is free to search out his beloved. All of that lives outside of the novel.

In the second ending, the meditation goes on for five pages, with the final page, numbered 168, in tatters, with the last few words torn away. On that final page of the second ending of *Old Keyam*, there is a discussion of a meeting in a ravine, reminiscent of the ending of *Black Hawk* when Allan Hawk and Helen meet on a bridge. In the second ending of *Old Keyam*, the state of the manuscript makes it difficult to make out several words, but it is clearly a musing on love:

> Maybe it is just XX trick of XXne [divine?], the real ones XXXse [pulse?] of those whose Xees [sees?] doth cultivate [a] taste for lovliness? [sic]
>
> Last night we went up the ravine that cuts in two the Hill. The frosted grXX [grasses?] like diamonds blinked, in a silvery woXXX at the Moon which hanged upon a cloud [no] breath of wind disturbed the frost that held intact, the atmosphere in its cold master grip. A beauty lay on either side, in Earth below and up the sky; but while my eyes beheld the sight, my heart oer flowed with joy. By that I see that what we are, within our inmost-selves—its what we are that makes us see and love things that are beautiful. A heart that's blunted by its grief or else by circumstance will pass a lovely sunset by, without a quickened throb.
>
> So then my heart rejoiced to sense the beauty of the night—the night that seems so big and pXXX [pure?]—the night that filled the universe with a darkening transparency. The heavenly eyes so far away blinked largely through the frost. The Great Bear all so prominent doth wink his seven-fold way and all seems richer than the day. No harrowed thoughts were in my heart. I shut its doors to all such things. What right have I an Indian born to feel the joys of Earth? A gulf is fixed? I dare to pass upon the wings of that Romance which once did sweep past me in flight. I may take flight across the chasm deep where is an alien life which long has had XXXXXXXX loved.[48]

What follows at the end of the final page of the *Old Keyam* manuscript are three words scratched out: "I have found"; then about two inches of paper has been torn away, with just enough detail that it is clear that there is more writing below. So, we really cannot determine his intended ending if this is, indeed, his intended last page.

In fact, long diagonal lines are discernible on each of the long pages of the second ending, indicating that it is all to be scrapped, even if in those five scrapped pages are some romantic musings.

It is, of course, tempting to link the ending of *Old Keyam* to *Black Hawk*, Ahenakew's novel, with the inconclusive ending. While we do not see Allan Hawk inheriting a pipe, we know he takes his responsibilities to his people very seriously. When he and Helen meet on the bridge in Winnipeg the first time, toward the end of the novel, Allan is quick to lay out his obligations:

> "There is one thing I'd like to talk to you about" he continued. "You may as well know it now as later. I said I belonged to my race and that was a solemn truth. I am theirs. I am not my own. All that is mine must ever be ready for service in the Cause of my people."[49]

While he has not been given a pipe, as Young Hawk was in the unpublished manuscript of *Old Keyam*, Allan Hawk feels a great devotion to his nation. It is on this point that Ahenakew's life is so similar.

When I first had the incredible privilege to read the handwriting of Ahenakew, his work hidden in the archives for so long, I was reminded of one of the first poems in Ahenakew's earliest notebook, about a dream he had about an ancestor that comes to him in a vision and tells him that he has led the youth astray. I thought about it alongside the image of the conflicted hero, burying the pipe he is bequeathed, poignant and evocative of the choice to abandon nêhiyaw spirituality, choices made by people in Ahenakew's generation.

However, since then I had the chance to talk to my cousin Lillian Sanderson, who is tasked by her First Nation to strategize so that a healing lodge can be built for the Lac La Ronge Indian Band. We were meeting over breakfast in the middle of the summer, and she shared how devastating the loss of Cree ways has been for our people. She said, in an off-hand way, having no way to know about Ahenakew's unpublished work, that buried all over the Prairies are pipes that have been abandoned by people who had no way to keep up cultural practices; they knew that to keep them would risk them falling into the wrong hands. I began to rethink my interpretation of the end of *Old Keyam*, when the Old Man Keyam wants to pass on the pipe to Young Hawk. Perhaps returning the pipe to the land was a way to protect it, when there was no other way to keep it safe.

ita kâ-ayâyahk pisiskêyihtâkwan kâ-isi-âcimohk

Our positions affect how a story is told

CHAPTER FIVE

How âcimisowin Preserves History
James Brady, Papaschase, and Absolom Halkett

Métis leader James Brady, one of the most important twentieth-century Indigenous political thinkers and activists in Canada, spoke English, French, and some Cree, and, was known to love books and reading.[1] Typically recognized as a successful political activist who, in the 1930s, worked with others to secure land rights for the Métis in Alberta, Brady spent the second half of his adult life in Saskatchewan.[2] His little cabin in La Ronge, Saskatchewan, was in the middle of the village and people would always mention that the inside walls were covered with books (with more of his collection stored in various other safe places[3]). His library was so large, with thousands of titles,[4] that this collection must have cost a lot of time and money to assemble.[5] And while some of the titles are well-known classics by Steinbeck, Tolstoy, or Djuna Barnes, a great deal of them are obscure titles of interest to eclectic readers like William Bolitho's *Twelve Against the Gods* and Elizabeth L. Wheaton's *Mrs. George's Joint*. In the holdings at the Glenbow Museum in Calgary, where dozens of boxes of Brady's papers are stored, are notes from publishing houses, confirming delivery of his orders for more books. There is even a list tucked into his October 1960 daybook with the names of friends and acquaintances and books listed under them, possibly a record of titles he lent to others.

There is also evidence that Brady studied literature. In a letter dated July 9, 1952, from the Toronto Writers Group, the secretary M. Holmes addresses "Mr. Brady" with the following: "I received your letter and request, and we are all interested in the fact that our Summer Course could arouse interest as far away from here as Stanley Mission" (not far from La Ronge). The secretary then encloses a reading list and discusses further information to come. Attached on the second page are lists of titles such as three books by Frederick Philip Grove and two by Hugh McLennan, with accompanying questions.[6]

But Brady wasn't just an avid reader. He wrote professionally. He wrote reports on social issues and organizational histories, and he kept regular correspondence with fellow political organizers. He was also a reliable researcher and translator. For example, a letter dated April 28, 1950, from Bruce Peel, who at the time was the curator for the Adam Shortt Collection of Canadiana at the University of Saskatchewan, provides some insight into Brady's skills. Peel thanks Brady for his translation of historian and sociologist Marcel Giraud's *Le métis canadien*, which quotes extensively from unpublished original trading post journals; Giraud's influential if flawed study was one of the first works on Métis history in existence, but initially was only available in French.[7] Peel lets Brady know that he is about to submit an essay to the journal *Saskatchewan History* and states: "In a footnote I shall acknowledge your assistance. I hope that if I should make any errors that you will write into the magazine correcting them."[8] Shortly thereafter, in 1951, Peel moved to the University of Alberta in Edmonton, first as a cataloguer, then deputy librarian, and finally "Librarian to the University."[9]

While this correspondence provides evidence that Brady knew Giraud's work on the Métis, there are also notes in Brady's archive that indicate his own ambitions to write a history himself.[10] In typed notes he lists out eighteen chapters of topics, beginning with notes for chapter one that call to mind Giraud's first chapter: "The Canadian West: The Physical Setting—Indigenous Society-Conception of Life and Psychology."[11] However, Brady planned to include history that Giraud barely mentions; in notes for chapter fifteen Brady lists "The Alberta Métis Association, 1928-1942—its work" as a topic to begin with; he then follows this with plans to write about the contributions of his four fellow activists that made up the Métis "Famous Five:—Sketches of J.F. Dion, Malcolm F. Norris, Peter C. Tomkins, and Felix Calihoo."[12]

Given this evidence that Brady wanted to write about the lives of his fellow organizers, it is not surprising that Brady wrote about his own life. To begin with, Brady was a committed diarist. Throughout his life he recorded events and his daily activities in a series of diaries.[13] He wrote daily during his war service: recording his location, sometimes the political situation, sometimes his own activities, logging news of people he knew, often listing casualties of the war. In comparison with peacetime, his wartime records are much more detailed, likely expanded as he created a document he called "Jottings from a Record of Service in the North West Europe Campaign July 9th 1944 - May 8th 1945."[14] Sometimes they were simply notes of where he was stationed and what the conditions were like, but sometimes drama peeks through. The fact that he typed up his handwritten journals indicates his ambitions to at least better preserve or make accessible his records, and perhaps also to find a readership.

From his archive, it is clear that Brady had ambitions to write a full autobiography. In the Brady fonds at the Glenbow Museum is a copy of a signed contract issued by A.K. Davis, the representative of the Center for

Community Studies, associated with the University of Saskatchewan, for Brady to produce "a life-history." The agreement was signed in Prince Albert by Davis and Brady on December 14, 1959. Also among his papers is a loose-leaf handwritten page, with the same date, presumably written by Davis and given to Brady that is titled "Suggestions for a life-history" and includes instructions to follow. The subjects underlined include: "the main phases of your life"; "images of self"; "roles"; "the significant others"; "institutions"; and "events." While there does not seem to be a full manuscript in his archive that follows these directions, Brady did complete a description of his birth.[15]

Brady describes the place he was born, in a little log shack near a lake that was originally known as Atimoswe Lake: "In the euphonious musical language of the Crees it was referred to as Dog Rump Lake. Our homestead stood on the second bench ... " He then writes:

> The night I was born was marked by a raging blizzard. My mother was alone. After hours of battering through the raging storm, my father and Dr. Charlebois, the early pioneer doctor of Northeast Alberta, reached me in a state of exhaustion. He was too late. Like William Blake I had sprung fearfully naked and bawling into the world of men.

In this passage Brady is referencing Blake's poem "Infant Sorrow," published in 1794 as part of Blake's *Songs of Experience*:

> My mother groaned, my father wept
> Into the dangerous world I leapt,
> Helpless, naked, piping loud,
> Like a fiend hid in a cloud.

That Brady is quoting from Blake is remarkable given that Blake was deemed a relatively minor poet until 1947, when Canadian literary critic Northrop Frye first published *Fearful Symmetry*, a study of Blake's poetry.[16] There is no evidence that Brady ever read Frye, but Blake's *Songs of Innocence and Experience*, which included "Infant Sorrow," is found in the inventory of his library.[17]

If the forty-three boxes of papers at the Glenbow are complete, then it appears that Brady never wrote more than that first chapter of his autobiography. However, his eleven-page manuscript entitled, "The Wisdom of Papasschayo, A Cree Medicine Man," is akin to another chapter of his âcimisowin. Ostensibly about a chief typically referred to as Papaschase, whose reserve lands were encroached upon by the city of Edmonton, it is also a rumination about Brady's family connection to their friend and neighbour.

It also records settlers' continuous encroachment on Indigenous lands. In 1906, the St. Paul Halfbreed Reserve (also known as St. Paul des Métis), where Brady's family was living before his birth, was taken over by white settlers—just as Papaschase's lands had been taken from his people fifteen years earlier, around the time of Edmonton's incorporation in 1892. The loss of his people's land, as well as the coming of three World Wars, had been foretold by Chief Papasschayo.[18]

Like Maria Campbell and Edward Ahenakew, who discuss their genealogies as a key part of their âcimisowina, Brady writes in various places about several ancestors and family members, especially his grandfather, Laurent Garneau, who had fought with Louis Riel. Brady catalogues the displacement of Papaschase's people and then of his own people. Woven throughout are the guidance and prophecies of Papaschase. While it is not a blood-family tie that Brady is emphasizing, he is demonstrating the kinship and respect he and his Métis family feel for this similarly displaced First Nation and the inter-relationship, the wâhkôhtowin, between himself and Papaschase. According to scholar Dwayne Donald, a descendent of the Papaschase Cree:

> Translated into English, wâhkôhtowin is generally understood to refer to kinship and relationality. In a practical way, wâhkôhtowin describes ethical guidelines regarding how you are related to your kin and how to conduct yourself as a good relative. The guidelines teach how to relate to human relatives and address them in accordance with traditional kinship teachings. However, wâhkôhtowin also refers to more-than-human kinship relations. The nêhiyaw worldview emphasizes honouring the ancient kinship and relationships that humans have with all other forms of life that comprise their traditional territories. This emphasis teaches human beings to understand themselves as fully enmeshed in networks of relationships that support and enable their life and living.[19]

In fact, Brady makes clear in his story about Chief Papaschase not only that his family is enmeshed with the Chief's family, but also with the land that they live upon together. He describes Papasschayo as a "rare combination of band chief and medicine man ... being possessed of clairvoyant and clairaudient powers," faced with violence from white settlers who want to take reserve land away from his people. Brady tells us that in 1892 Papaschase takes time to consider his band's options in the face of the threat by the settlers. He directs his people to leave their territory to avoid bloodshed, saying, "We must find the pathway that leads to the stars"; the band then moves west to the Rocky Mountains.

Brady then shares another story about a time his family visits Papaschase circa 1906, when their own community—the St. Paul Halfbreed Reserve—was under threat. Papaschase spends some days praying and fasting, confirms that Brady's community will lose their land, and then prophesies about three great wars; the first would break out in ten years' time, another a generation later, and then a last great battle because "the Paleface is never satisfied. He wants everything under the sun."[20]

Brady sought publication for this work; he reached out to anthropologist Charles Brant from the Department of Sociology and Anthropology at the University of Alberta for feedback. On May 6, 1963, in a letter on Department letterhead, Charley[21] discusses Brady's submission of what he calls "Legend of Pappasschayo [sic]."[22] Charley does not believe Brady's description of the Chief's powers to predict the future:

> My hunch would be that, although Papaschayo [sic] was an illiterate Indian without knowledge of any European language, the circumstances of life and of those times were such that, in all probability, he had heard others talking about the tide of events in Europe preceding the first World War.[23]

And Charley is also critical of supernatural beliefs in any form:

> You are right in assuming that my scientific training and attendant skepticism makes me tend to reject occult explanations of anything. But as historical materialists I think this view is incumbent upon us. Can we, for instance, reject the "pie in the sky" Christian view of life and after-life as nonsense and political dope-peddling—but at the same time, accept occultistic, supernaturalistic explanations of events by medicine-men, just because the latter are Indians, Africans, Australian aboriginals, or whatever? I think we have to be consistent.

Brady still submitted the manuscript to the *Alberta Historical Review* and received further criticism about the manuscript, for different reasons. On December 10, 1963, editor Hugh Dempsey writes: "As a historian, I am obliged to consider any manuscripts in the cold light of recorded facts. While I am sure the traditions of your family have been faithfully recorded in the manuscript, they do not completely agree with the official records."[24] In the case of Dempsey, he does not mention the "occult" incidents but instead believes the critique of how the reserve fell into the hands of settlers is incorrect: "The whole matter of the surrender and sale of the Passpasschase [sic] Reserve has been a murky one and was likely accompanied by a certain amount of graft and corruption. However, it is still a fact that the Reserve had been legally surrendered by the time the railroad came and that the land was already falling into the hands of white settlers." Dempsey then writes, "I am truly sorry that we cannot use the manuscript."[25]

It is so common for Indigenous authors to aspire to the publication of material they are uniquely qualified to write, only to have it rejected with the explanation that their work is deficient or unbelievable. Two other Indigenous authors and peers of Brady also tried to publish âcimisowina, marked by community history. Fellow activist Joseph Dion tried to have *My Tribe, the Crees* published in his lifetime; likewise, fellow veteran Mike Mountain Horse tried to publish *My People, the Bloods*. Both texts were rejected by publishers. In an odd twist of fate, their work was edited and published in 1979, after both of their deaths, by Hugh Dempsey himself.

Once Brady and his prospecting partner went missing without a trace in June 1967, his books and papers were gathered up by his executor, Allan Quandt. Among these papers was a list, typed out by Brady, of a record of his entire library. When Brady's will was probated a decade later, an inventory was made of all his materials. In a letter to Kathy Quandt dated August 7, 1975, Ken Hatt, from the Department of Sociology at the University of Alberta in Edmonton, identified features of Brady's archive, including the list of books that had over 4,400 titles.[26]

As far as we can tell by the material available, Brady did not leave behind any works longer than those discussed above.[27] But Brady continues to be remembered because of his mysterious disappearance in June 1967. I always knew about this mystery, as various versions circulated around during my childhood. And I thought of Brady as more than an historical figure because I knew that he and Malcolm Norris worked with Uncle Frank's dad in Alberta in the 1930s, resulting in a lifelong friendship between Jim and Frank. But I didn't think there were any other connections with our family until a visit with Uncle Frank and Auntie Irene in 2002.

I had just finished a trip to La Ronge and was mulling over family stories. I was thinking about how my grandmother had cured a man of blindness. I had just had a conversation with my uncle about kôhkum's dream about the bear, which directed her to collect the right medicine. I was stumped by the idea that Uncle Vic didn't know this part of the story. When I stopped in Saskatoon to have tea with my Auntie Irene, I asked her right away if this detail was, as I remembered, the part of the story that was always told. "Of course," she said.

Uncle Frank overheard us, asked us what we were talking about, and I said, "Oh you know, that story ... the one about Absolom Halkett." Frank looked curiously at me and said, "Why would you ask her about Abbie Halkett when I'm the one who knows the most about this?" I sat there stunned and uncomprehending. It's true that Uncle Frank's mother and kôhkom were both healers and friends, but he grew up in Alberta and only went to Northern Saskatchewan as an adult. How could he know more about this story of healing than Irene?

"You know about Jim Brady, don't you?" he asked, and I did know about the work James Brady and Malcolm Norris had done as Métis leaders in Northern Saskatchewan because I had read up on them at some point.[28] My parents had, as newlyweds, camped with Brady and Norris in La Ronge. Through Mom I had heard that in June 1967 he and another man were dropped off by plane at Lower Foster Lake, about 300 kilometres north of La Ronge so that they could go prospecting. When their boss flew in a week later to replenish their supplies, their camp was set up, their boat was tied near the shore, but they were missing without a trace.[29]

I wasn't sure how Absolom Halkett fit into the equation. "This is a story I've always wanted to see come to the light," Uncle Frank told me.

> You know Malcolm Norris was Métis but he could get away with looking white. He was working with a bunch of S.O.B.s as a prospector. Now Abbie Halkett was a full-blooded Indian and looked like one, and so did Jim Brady. But Malcolm said that if these white men wanted to work with him, they also had to work with Abbie and Jim. Well just about the time that Malcolm got pretty sick I saw Abbie and Jim getting ready to go and establish a claim. The word was out that they had struck it rich and even splitting the pot five ways, there was going to be plenty of money to go around.[30]

So Brady's prospecting partner was none other than Absolom Halkett, the man kôhkom had cured of blindness. Uncle Frank told me that the two white partners knew that Norris was too sick to fight for Jim and Abbie, and besides being racist they were greedy. He said that they must have hired thugs to fly up from the States who, using the pretense that they were on a hunting trip, made sure that Jim and Abbie would never be seen again.[31] According to Uncle Frank, once Norris passed away, the two partners made a bundle.

I thanked Uncle Frank for telling me this story. As I think back over the stories that Mom shared with me, I don't think she ever told me that the same man who was healed by kôhkom from blindness was the one who went missing with Jim.

I do remember Mom telling me other things about their disappearance, though. Mom said that at some point the police had determined that Jim and Abbie had gotten lost, or even more implausibly, that Jim and Abbie had intentionally tried to walk out of the bush, points that made her exhale with exasperation. Anyone who knows the terrain in Northern Saskatchewan knows the bush and muskeg and water that begins about an hour outside of Saskatoon, around Prince Albert, and extends north. It is unthinkable that anyone who knew that land would try to walk out, especially when they knew that their boss was scheduled to fly in by plane to replenish their supplies and check in on them within the week.[32]

Sometimes Mom would tell me that even though the RCMP called off the search a couple of weeks after the disappearance, Jim and Abbie's friends and community members continued to look for them all summer. And except for a few clues like a scuff mark on a rock wall, the 1967 community search team found nothing. When I asked Mom what happened to Jim and Abbie, she told me that the UFOs must have taken them. That seemed more logical than any of the theories I had heard up until then.

For Frank it was clear that Jim and Abbie had been murdered, either for their politics or by corrupt business partners who wanted to cut Jim and Abbie out of a claim. Regardless, he was convinced that whoever the murderer was, they would have dropped the bodies into Lower Foster Lake, and that the lake was so cold that the bodies were likely still there and intact. This was a story that Frank told me often over the years, sharing his theories in great detail.

After Irene passed on in 2005, I visited Frank in Saskatoon several times, sometimes alone or sometimes with family. Usually my cousin Connie was there, helping her dad, and in recent years my cousin Pat too. In summer 2016, Frank, at this point almost ninety years old, called me explicitly to come to visit him so that we could strategize how to find Jim and Abbie.

I know that Uncle Frank thought of me as a researcher and was really proud when I finished my doctoral dissertation. He was confident that I would have the skills to take the lead on the search. But what I left unsaid, that I expected was too obvious a point to have to state out loud, is that while I have been able to find documents written by Indigenous authors hidden in archives, no one would ever think that I have any skills to find bodies hidden in lakes. While I can organize literary awards, I do not have the ability to lead searches on land or under water. No one would mistake me for an outdoorswoman. I knew that if I had endless amounts of time, I could research anything, but I was already too busy and not sure where to begin. Still, I did what I could with my limited skill set. I wrote out a research plan that included hiring an underwater search team, with as much confidence as if I had sketched out a plan to fly to the moon. I tried to figure out how to proceed.

Little did I know that key factors needed for this search would after half a century fall so easily in place. One of my cousins, Eric Bell, besides being a member of Parks Canada for a few decades before he established an ambulance service in La Ronge, is incredibly skilled on the land and with people. He is part of the same First Nation as Abbie Halkett, and as a boy he remembers Jim Brady visiting our grandparents' home, called "the Brown house," presumably because of its colour, and talking politics with our grandfather. When Eric neared the age of retirement, he found himself with more time than he had ever had before, and when I told him about Uncle Frank's insistence that I search for Jim and Abbie, he was intrigued by a mystery that he had always known.

Eric also knew Thompson Mackenzie and Stanley Roberts, two community members who lived in nearby Grandmother's Bay, which is part of the Lac La Ronge Indian Band. While Stanley is too young to remember the disappearance, Eric and Thompson distinctly remember the community suspicion, which has continued for years, that Jim and Abbie had met with foul play. Because Jim and Abbie were politically active, there was a hesitancy by the community to trust the authorities, who might have been happy to see two Indigenous leaders disappear.

Eric knew that Thompson and Stanley operated a sonar unit, and they had become experts in underwater searches. Eric also knew that on Lower Foster Lake there is a Fly-in Fishing Lodge, so that if we wanted to gather a search party, it would be relatively easy to plan a trip, since the lodge could provide the flight there, along with cabins, meals, boats, and pontoons on which to operate the sonar.

Around this time I had met a new friend, Australian researcher Michael Nest, who has expertise in archival research and anti-corruption work in the mining sector. When I learned that his partner was accepted into graduate school in Montreal, requiring them to relocate to Canada, suddenly Michael was close enough to invite him into the project. I began to tell him about Uncle Frank and Jim and Abbie, partly because the fiftieth anniversary of their disappearance was looming and partly because it is the quintessential Canadian story to tell a newcomer. Two Indigenous men, well-known in their community and in the prime of their lives, go out onto the land for work and vanish. The authorities conduct a cursory investigation, posit that it was the fault of the missing, decide the location is too isolated to continue the search, and determine that the case is unsolved and likely unsolvable. Eventually, mainstream Canada does not remember Jim or Abbie or that they disappeared.

Without a doubt Eric and Michael are two ideal search partners. Eric is as comfortable on the lake as he is on land, and except for the years in residential school or college, he has spent his entire life in the north, so that he knows pretty much everybody, or at least every family, in La Ronge and the surrounding areas. Any historical figure that we had questions about, Eric knew a way to reach out. And Michael is an insatiable, detailed, ethical researcher and elegant writer. It is Eric who is to be credited with helping find even more pieces of the puzzle, as community members continue to share what they know. Credit for the book that came out of the search goes to Michael, who wrote most of it, driven by his curiosity and devotion to this case.

It has been a long process. As part of our research, we made several trips together, including to Saskatchewan and to the James Brady fonds at the Glenbow Museum and Archives in Calgary, to gather as much information as possible before we scheduled our first lake search in August 2018. At some point Michael and I stopped at the site of Jim's cabin, where I had vague childhood memories of visits to this location because my Uncle George and Auntie Jane had lived next door. We then went up the road to the local Native Friendship Centre and saw that the Métis local had put up a statue in memory of Jim Brady. It's a handsome monument and so we read carefully the text engraved upon it, thinking about the legacy of this talented, amazing man.

We immediately realized that the wording was odd. The monument stated that Jim went missing in 1967 with "his Cree friend." Given that Abbie Halkett was also from La Ronge, a band councillor with the Lac La Ronge Indian Band, and with family still in the area, it seemed such an indignity that in that moment of memorial, Abbie's name would be forgotten, something that Jim would not do. I began to realize that a lot of the documents about Brady going missing often refer to an unnamed Cree partner.

Shortly thereafter we travelled with Eric, Thompson, and Stanley to Lower Foster Lake. Eric drove the lodge pontoon backwards so that Michael could help Thompson feed out the line of the sonar "starfish"; the sonar then sent images to the laptop screen, and Stanley monitored it, looking for anomalies.[33] Thompson also played the role of counsellor or Elder. He would remind us to take seriously the work we were doing and to express the emotions that resulted from the search. I still remember the early mornings on the search days, when I was still asleep in bed, the lonely feeling that came over me as I dreamt that Jim and Abbie were curled up just like me, as if asleep, but lying on the lake bottom.

At some point, when we were together at the lodge for dinner, Michael and I shared the story of the error on the monument for Jim. "Can you imagine why they wouldn't bother finding out the name of the so-called "Cree friend?" I ranted. "That's all right," said Stanley, a smart, quiet young man known for his wit. "The Lac La Ronge Indian band office is going to put up a statue of Abbie Halkett," he declared, "and write below it that he went missing with his Métis friend." I still laugh when I think about his dry delivery and our immediate smiles in response. I began to realize that the story my mother told me, about the time kôhkom cured a man named Absolom Halkett from blindness, has helped keep Abbie's name remembered.

Sometimes, stories can keep within them the disquiet of something that has gone wrong, the memory of a trauma. In 1913, when my kôhkom and her brother Baptiste were away at residential school, her mother, my câpân, was with family in Sled Lake while kôhkom's father, Cornelius Durocher, went downriver to Prince Albert. A newspaper article at the time reported that a seriously injured man that they identified as Cornelius De Rosier, from Green Lake, "was said to be one of an Indian wedding party who were in the city ... "

The family story is that he was playing cards under the bridge in Prince Albert, gambling for money. Everyone who has told me the story is very clear that he was gambling with members of the police. He was winning, and so, they told me, the police killed him.

The article on page one of the April 5, 1913 edition of the *Shellbrook Chronicle* has a different version. The headline states: "Fell Through Bridge" and said that a man "was discovered here below the C.N.R. Bridge this morning." It continues:

> Upon examination it was found that the man was suffering from a compound fracture of both legs and was bleeding profusely.
>
> Dr. Bliss was sent for and ordered his removal to the Holy Family Hospital, where he lays in a precarious condition.... It is supposed that he fell through a gap between the railway track and the roadway while crossing the bridge during the night.

I have two other documents that mentions this accident. The first is the Certificate of Cause of Death that states that Cornelius Durocher died due to "legs broken" and the date is seemingly a guess: "the beginning of the month of May 1913 and by the end of May." The document is signed by Rev J. E. Teston, o.m.i., which would be Reverend Jules Emile Teston, of the Missionary Oblates of the Mary Immaculate at Green Lake.[34] In the line that asks for the name of the attending physician, Teston has written: "I don't know him." It is clear then that, besides the report in the newspaper, no one filled out any further documentation until my great-grandfather's body was returned to Green Lake.

The second document that I have is his Registration of Death, also signed by Teston, which was dated the 15th of December 1913 and accepted in Prince Albert by the registrar on the 26th of December 1913. This backdated document states that Cornelius Durocher died on the 1st of May 1913; this indicates that even though Cornelius Durocher died in Prince Albert in early May, no one in Prince Albert filled out the official documents at the time of his death.

I have not been able to find any documentation about my great-grandfather's time spent in the Holy Family hospital, what happened to him between his accident in early April and then his passing in May. Neither is there an official explanation as to how it is that his registration of death might be so delayed. But my Uncle Vic told me that when Cornelius Durocher was killed, he was buried in a pauper's grave.

At the time of my great-grandfather's death, his daughter/my kôhkom, was about ten years of age and enrolled in residential school. Even though it was decided that kôhkom's younger brother would stay until the end of the school year, kôhkom was called home to Green Lake to be with her mother, my câpân. There are no stories about çâpân getting the chance to travel to Prince Albert, so that she could see her husband before his death. And it caused the family some consternation when they discovered that the body had been interred with strangers, so far from home.

According to Uncle Vic, it was determined that câpân's uncle, Moise, John Mirasty's son, would be able to locate and bring home the body of my great-grandfather. Moise made the trip to Prince Albert, and after dealing with the authorities, exhumed Cornelius Durocher, put him in a coffin, and returned him to Green Lake to be buried.

This small story is a part of a terrible history in my family of unexpected and unexplained deaths. But even without official explanations or convictions, and even with a suspicion that authorities did not give appropriate attention, these stories affirmed that relatives and communities cared. Even if there were times that we couldn't do much, there was always a collective concern that didn't dissipate quickly, and this feeling of loss and connection transferred from one generation to the next.

Uncle Frank had told me that over the years he had been in touch with both the families of Jim Brady and Abbie Halkett. While Michael and I had sought out permission from both Jim and Abbie's daughters as we began our research, it was Frank who shared with us how he had been in contact for years with one of Abbie's granddaughters and so knew first-hand from her how much she and her family missed him. They yearned for evidence of his life. It made us realize that while there is a robust archive that has been preserved about and by Jim, finding information about and images of Abbie has been more difficult.

In our research we eventually were able to locate four photographs, and we sought permission from their owners to share them so that Abbie's grandchildren and family would be able to see them. Because we were aware that we were researching a tragedy, we worked cautiously, constantly confirming with families involved that we had ongoing permission to continue. We were reassured when Abbie's granddaughter reached out by social media to share how happy she was to see images of the grandfather she never met.

Our sense of wâhkôhtowin led us to know that we had to walk cautiously, because to add to any hurt of her would only add to our own, and likewise her joy would add to our joy. With this sense of obligation to Abbie and his family, we continued our search to collect stories about him. We already knew, from the story Mom had told me all those years ago, that Abbie had wanted to become an Anglican minister; as we researched, we realized that this was a career choice made by a lot of Cree intellectuals in Saskatchewan in the first half of the twentieth century, bright minds like Edward Ahenakew, like Stan Cuthand. We also found reference to Abbie's intelligence in the oral archive. In a 1976 interview, a longtime La Ronge resident, Gwendoline Beck, described Abbie as "a young fellow that went out to Indian Residential schools, was very brilliant, and went on to university."[35] Even though he never became a minister, Abbie did serve as a schoolteacher for a time, and then as a band councillor. This ended shortly before he went out on his last trip prospecting with Jim. In a 1978 interview, community organizer Liora Salter

Fig. 5 Left to right: Isabel Tomkins, Victoria Patterson (kôhkom), Judy Zigler, and Francoise Merasty Durocher Morin (câpân). In front: Janet Patterson, c.1980. Reder family photo.

remembered Abbie as "definitely a political person."[36] By the 1967 disappearance, Abbie was 39 years old, two decades younger than Jim.

There was one more story of Abbie that I was able to find, one more story to connect with others as an example of âniskwâcimopicikêwin. On Thanksgiving in 2005, my husband and I flew to Edmonton for my cousin Lindsay's wedding. When we arrived at the reception, I saw Uncle Vic standing to the side, and I realized that I hadn't visited with him since our last trip to La Ronge a few years earlier. I remembered how he had shared with me that while he knew that his mom had cured Abbie of blindness, he had never heard the accompanying story about kôhkom's dream of a bear whose neck was entangled in medicines.

I wanted him to know that I had followed up with Auntie Irene, and she had confirmed that she had heard the same version of the story that my mom had told me. "Why, I wonder," I asked Uncle Vic, "was this part of the story never shared with you?" He answered easily, as though he had been thinking about this for a while. "What you don't understand is that when we were growing up, we were told that the Indian stuff was no good and that the white man's things were better."

"But you know," he continued, "there were lots of things that happened that you wouldn't believe. And there was medicine like that that you had to be careful with," he told me. "You know Abbie Halkett, he went to school, he was educated. An old man from Stanley Mission came to him, just like you would do in the old days, and told Abbie that he wanted him to marry his daughter. Abbie was going to be a minister, he didn't know what to say, but he didn't want to marry her this way. That upset the old man, who cursed him and told Abbie, 'You're going to become blind.'"

awîna mwêhci kiya?

Who is it that you really are?

CHAPTER SIX

kiskêyihtamowin
Seekers of Knowledge, Cree Intergenerational Inquiry,
Shared by Harold Cardinal

My parents were wary of school. It is not that they did not embrace formal education, but rather that it did not embrace them.

My mother attended a small school in the village of La Ronge, on the shore of the lake of the same name. From all of her stories, there are two about going to school in the 1940s and 50s that she often repeated to me. The first was about the best mark she ever received, something significant because she wasn't used to receiving good grades and praise.

At some point in her elementary school years, she was assigned to write an essay on any subject matter that she wished. She decided to describe how to prepare for a winter on the trapline, something she knew about because she had accompanied her parents out trapping since she was five years of age and even as a girl could skin and clean any animal. She wrote out each step and handed it in and was surprised and proud that she received an "A" for her work. This was a story I could easily imagine because, when I was a child, my grandparents still trapped. We would stay with them at their summer camp at Eight-and-a-Half, and my mother and grandparents would visit in a mixture of Cree and English. I would follow kôhkom around as she collected medicines, but I could not talk with her because I didn't speak the language. It seemed to me that you would need to know how a whole different world worked to live in this place.

The second story my mother would tell explained why she quit school at the end of grade nine. She described how she had to memorize the names of the kings and queens of England, complete with their dates of succession to the throne. She never could get it straight. One day she decided not to go to class but instead went to the local café to apply to be a waitress. When they gave her the job on the spot, she effectively ended her schooling.

At some point, Mom moved south to work in cafés in Regina and live with her sister, Helen. Then she moved to Manitoba to work in the diet kitchen of a tuberculosis sanatorium. About the same time, one of her brothers, my

Fig. 6 At Frank and Irene's wedding, c. 1965. Left to right: Frank Tomkins, Bella Bell, Adele Tomkins, and Vicky Patterson. Reder family photo.

uncle Ray, joined the Princess Patricia's Canadian Light Infantry and was stationed in Shiloh, less than an hour away from where Mom worked. When he came to visit her, he brought a fellow soldier along. It ended up that Dad wasn't a complete stranger to the family. His best friend at that time was Jimmy Tomkins, whose little brother Frank ended up marrying my auntie Irene. Dad would go hunting or drinking with them sometimes.

Mom used to say that she was disappointed at first with my Dad's blonde hair and blue eyes but that he grew on her. Six months later they got married, and I was born a few years after that in a nearby Brandon hospital. Dad was born in 1933 in St. Owen's, Manitoba, the child of German-speaking Poles who had arrived in the 1920s after the First World War. Dad's only memory of his school years that he talked about took place when he was thirteen years old and in grade six. He got into trouble with the teacher—the only detail mentioned about her was that she was a redhead—and she decided to strap him on the hands until he repented. He refused to cry in front of his classmates, and this infuriated her so much that she beat him, losing count after 20 lashes on each hand, until his hands were masses of welts. Dad didn't tell me that in fact this story "mushroomed into an issue of province-wide concern" when the teacher was charged with lashing him 104 times. "Miss Kristianson claimed that half the number named would be closer to the truth."[1] It seemed that Dad broke her rule about not eating sunflower seeds in the classroom. Even though a picture of Dad and the teacher made it into the local newspaper under the headline "Strapping Stirs Tempest" with the note that they were now the "best of friends," Dad didn't return for grade seven but instead worked in logging camps until he was seventeen and old enough to join the army.

For whatever reason my experience in school was completely different. I loved the books and the tests and the praise, which both pleased and mystified my parents. Given that my brother, who has multiple disabilities, was placed in special programs, my success at school was unusual in my family, and I quickly concluded that my life in school had no relation to my life at home. It never surprised me when my family didn't understand what I wanted to do or learn or think about. I studied the bible, the history of the royal families of England and Monaco, the classics of English literature, and biographies of people like Marie Curie and Helen Keller.

Yet even though I loved to read and write, and it was easy to describe my life at school, I knew that describing my family in words did not put us in the best of light, something I knew was wrong and complicated. Part of this was context. School was an easy space to reference because everyone could imagine the classroom with a teacher at the front near a blackboard, with classmates all about the same age and books and tests and bells that rang to mark the passing of time. Central to my mother's stories was the place where she grew up, where much of the family still lived and where those of us who lived away would reunite. But describing La Ronge to my classmates was difficult for me to do. In those days we would have to drive to Saskatoon, then Prince Albert, and then head north for about five hours, over a gravel road. When we arrived, dusty and shaken, we were in a world that was completely unlike the almost-suburban order of the private military quarters of the army bases we lived on.

What was particularly disturbing and difficult to explain was that even though this place resembled the stories of my mother's childhood—the water barrels, the piles of firewood for the woodstoves, the outhouses—by the 1970s, there was something new that didn't exist in Mom's recountings, a sense of lawlessness that seemed to be inescapable. When I was seven, my teenage cousins took me shoplifting with them and then took me into the bush to drink the stolen bottles of pop. The afternoon matinee on Main Street would let children in to see whatever show was playing, and I would sit confused, watching movies that were rated R.

But other, worse things happened. Two of my beautiful and talented aunties passed away unexpectedly, leaving behind small children. Strong old ladies, the mothers and grandmothers of large families, would spend nights in the drunk tank. I remember my mother telling me that people didn't use to drink so heavily.

And disasters happened regularly. My cousin Richard Bell, sweet-natured and well-known by everyone, with disabilities like my brother's, was found dead at the bottom of the stairs of the La Ronge hotel. Even though his death was highly suspicious, no one was ever charged.

All this to me was part of being Cree, being Métis, and I didn't really have a language to talk about it. I did not expect when I went to university that I would find a vocabulary there that would help me understand what was happening because my education was, in my mind, completely separate from being a member of my family. True to my expectations, in my history course on Canada I learned a lot about "the founding of the nation" and nothing about "Native peoples." There were no courses on Native literatures, what we called it back then, or even books by Native authors. I never had an Indigenous professor and, in literature classes anyway, there were no other Indigenous students, as far as I could tell. So segregated were my two worlds that this did not seem strange to me.

Around 1988 I had the chance to hear Abenaki poet and National Film Board Director Alanis Obomsawin give a talk at Concordia University in Montreal. I remember being both so impressed and surprised by what she had to say that I went up after her talk to ask her if it was actually true, were there really books written by Native authors. It seems to me in retrospect that this question was not as odd and embarrassing as I came to remember it. At that point I had been an avid reader who had gone to libraries regularly for almost half of my life. At eleven, I had my first paper route, and I have read the daily paper ever since.

Because my Dad had been stationed at several different military bases across western Canada, and because I had taken part in a youth program called Katimavik, by 1988 I had lived in or spent extended time visiting eight of the ten provinces. I listened to the CBC. By the time I heard Obomsawin, I had completed two years of university. Yet none of these practices regularly associated with broadening one's mind—reading, being aware of current events, travelling, higher education—had given me any indication of the accomplishments of Indigenous authors. None of this taught me a history of Canada that I could recognize.

Things changed shortly after this when Indigenous authors were beginning to publish. In the late 1980s, Drew Hayden Taylor, Daniel David Moses, and Tomson Highway began their careers as playwrights.[2] Armand Ruffo,

Kateri Akiwenzie-Damm, Marilyn Dumont, Thomas King, Eden Robinson, Richard Van Camp and Richard Wagamese released their first books.[3] By the mid-1990s, even though I was no longer in school, I was thrilled and inspired by the productions by Cree and Métis artists: Tomson Highway, Gregory Scofield, Louise Halfe. I came across the stories collected by Cree linguist Freda Ahenakew, and listened to Tom King's Jasper and Gracie from the *Dead Dog Café*, speaking Cree regularly on CBC Radio. In 2000 I took the only course in the Department of English at the University of British Columbia on Indigenous literatures, and began a PhD in the following year.[4]

Because there were no other Indigenous students in the doctoral program in the Department of English, I gravitated to the First Nations House of Learning, a gathering space for Indigenous students at my university, many who juggled their studies as I did around our children and family commitments.[5] It was also there, on xʷməθkʷəy̓əm (Musqueam) land, that I learned the value of following Coast Salish protocols. When speaking in a group, we were taught to introduce ourselves in relation to our families and to the land and its peoples. Coast Salish people, for example, would identify themselves, including the names of their parents and communities, and if applicable, by ceremonial names often linked to the ancestors. Those of us who were not from these lands were taught to introduce ourselves by our families and nations and the territories where we were from, and to acknowledge that despite our length of time in the area, we did not have the same relationship with this place as the host First Nations did.

It was during this time that I became aware of cultural differences between First Nations. While anthropologists might have coined the term "Coast Salish" to describe dozens of groups that live all along the West Coast of the United States and Canada, even those closely located to each other, the xʷməθkʷəy̓əm, Tsleil-Waututh, and Skwxwú7mesh Peoples, for example, consider themselves to be related but separate nations.[6] It was during this time that I came to understand that local songs can be owned by individual families and use of the songs is considered private, unless families have given permission for them to be used by others.[7] In comparison, in sweatlodges that were run by Métis ceremonialist Madeline McIvor and nêhiyaw/anishinaabe medicinalist Alannah Young, I learned that the teachings of the Medicine Wheel, derived from ceremonial practices of Prairie nations, while structured around strict protocols, are considered to be more open to participation by visitors.[8]

I began to think about the concerns around protocol in relation to my own work. What are my responsibilities as a Cree-Métis scholar to respect the tradition of the land on which I am a guest? What principles should govern my intellectual work? What obligations do I have to scholars from other nations, or to those from my own? While these questions seem to lie outside the purview of conventional literary studies, in the field of Indigenous literary studies Osage scholar Robert Warrior reminds us of the need to participate in work that "can contribute to improving the intellectual health of Native America, its people, and its communities."[9]

In March 2005, I had the honour to hear eminent Cree lawyer and leader Harold Cardinal speak at UBC's First Nations House of Learning in one of his last public talks.[10] I will always remember this lecture, entitled "Einew Kis-Kee-Tum-Awin."[11] Because Cardinal had been struggling with his final illness, his voice was weak. He spoke each phrase and paused so that his wife Maisie could then repeat his words.

In his address, Cardinal begins by arguing that proficiency in Cree is necessary to fully understand a term such as "einew kiss-kee-tum-awin," spelled in Standard Roman Orthography as iyiniw kiskêyihtamowin, which means "Indigenous People's Knowledge." Cardinal states:

> It is a concept rooted in the language and conceptual framework of the Cree people. It is a term, which incorporates many different, complex and complicated, though inter-related terms and concepts each originating from and rooted in the Cree language and Cree belief systems.[12]

Cardinal then explains that Elders and Cree traditions "support and sustain any institutions we create." He gives an example:

> Many years ago a Cree Elder asked me the following question: awina maga kiya[13]—who is it that you really are?[14] I replied in Cree—neehiyow neyah[15]—at the time I thought I was saying "I am an Indian."[16]

While Cardinal believed that nêhiyaw niya means "I am an Indian," the Elder pushes him to think more deeply about this answer, and to encourage Cardinal to think about what it means to be Cree, or "nêhiyaw," instead of an "Indian."

It is not surprising that a young Harold Cardinal would think about himself in the more general term. In the vernacular of the time, as well as in the autobiography and non-fiction writing of that era, it was common for Indigenous people to refer to themselves as Indians: *I am an Indian* (1969);[17] *The Only Good Indian* (1970);[18] edited by Waubageshig; Lee Maracle's *Bobbi Lee, Indian Rebel* (1975), and of course, Cardinal's own *The Unjust Society: The Tragedy of Canada's Indians* (1969). There was logic to his translation. However, the Elder wants to challenge Cardinal's sense of what it means to be nêhiyaw. The Elder asks in Cree:

"ta ni ki maga nee hi youw kee tig a wee yin? tansi ee twee maga?[19] Why is it that you are called 'neehiyow'—what does the word mean?" When the Elder realized that I did not fully understand the meaning of the word "neehiyow," the Elder proceeded to explain.... The Elder said:

The word "Neehiyow" comes from two words in our language: (1) Neewoo [nêwo]—Four and (2) Yow [wiyaw]—Body [World]. In the context in which I use the term, it means: Four Worlds or Four Bodies. We believe that the Creator placed knowledge in each of the Four Worlds. These are the sources of knowledge, which our people must seek to understand so that both their spiritual and physical survival will grow and continue. When we say that "I am a Neehiyow" what I really am saying is that I come from "the people who seek the knowledge of the Four Worlds." In short when I apply the word "Neehiyow" to myself, what I am saying is that "I am a seeker of knowledge."

It is not coincidental that Cardinal uses an autobiographical anecdote in his discussion of Cree philosophy. Not only does it construct him as a student, but it also places the Elder in the position of teacher and emphasizes the cooperative element in the Cree search for knowledge. In Cree thought, according to Cardinal, one's identity is not peripheral but rather central to any form of intellectual work. Cardinal continues:

Neehiyow [nêhiyaw] Elders recognized that the four worlds contained such enormous sources of knowledge that even a person's lifetime was not long enough in which to gather and understand the knowledge, which was there. Hence they saw the pursuit of knowledge as an unending, continuous inter-generational exercise in which one generation would pass onto the next generation, the knowledge which had been gathered and understood with the expectation that subsequent generations would continue the inter-generational process of gathering and understanding knowledge.

Throughout the eons of time preceding the arrival of the White man to our land and territories, our peoples evolved, developed, maintained and sustained complex systems through which they continued the knowledge quest.[20]

In these teachings, cooperation is undeniably a significant part of intellectual work. Because there is more knowledge than anyone can hope to learn in one lifetime, people must work together. This means that seekers must not only cooperate with and respect their companions but also work with what is left to them by the generations before them. This concept of intergenerational inquiry is not limited to learning what previous generations knew but also appreciates the role of subsequent generations. Rather than limit the search for knowledge to the intellectual sphere, Cree understandings include the physical, the spiritual, and the emotional.[21]

Fascinatingly, there is a challenge to this Elder's story, although not to the teachings per se.[22] It is without a doubt that in Cree four is a sacred number and that knowledge transmission must take into consideration the work of ancestors and descendants. What has been disputed by fully fluent Cree speaker, linguist, and lexicographer, Kevin Brousseau, is the etymology of the word nêhiyaw. He contends that the word "nêwo," the number four, does not exist in the word nêhiyaw. Brousseau states that:

> If this were the case, we would expect to find evidence either in the historical record or in another dialect or related language, yet no evidence for this can be found anywhere. No such word exists in any Cree dialect or related language.[23]

Linguistics aside, the story that Cardinal shares is about himself as a young man, born in 1945, who thinks of himself as a colonial subject, an Indian. Cree teacher Solomon Ratt—with a similar upbringing to Cardinal, born less than a decade after him—shares the negative associations of growing up as "Indian" during that time. Ratt tells a wawiyatâcimowina, a funny little story about his own childhood when he and his fellow residential school inmates would mimic the storylines in movies by playing "Cowboys and Indians" on the playground:

> That's how we used to play, and at that time as we were growing up we really used to, uh ... we had a poor opinion of ourselves. We used to be told that we shouldn't live like Cree people, that's the way we were raised there at that school.

Schooled in this self-hatred that was supported by popular culture, Ratt shares a moment in their game:

> But this one time we were going to watch this Cowboys and Indi-ans movie, and it had John Wayne in it. I liked it. I really enjoyed watching those ones, I liked to watch those, to watch John Wayne. Then when we had finished watching those ones, we used to go to play Cowboys and Indians and we'd gather ourselves together [choosing sides]. Ah, on one side were the Indians and the other were the Cowboys. And I used to always be the one chosen last. Well eventually on this one day I came to be chosen, and apparently I was

supposed to be an Indian. Oh, I didn't like that, I really didn't want to be considered an Indian.

"I'm not an Indian," I said. "I'm not going to be an Indian."[24]

It is clear in Ratt's story that as a child he wants to disassociate himself from the negative ramifications of being Indian, especially being relegated to the losing side in Hollywood battles. And in Cardinal's story, situated in a similar historical context as Ratt, the Elder wants to encourage Cardinal to reject the negative associations with an identity as merely "Indian." Instead, the Elder asks Cardinal to rethink and reimagine what it means to be nêhiyaw, in order to inspire him to associate being Cree with the search for knowledge. Given Cardinal's astounding role as a leading nêhiyaw legal theorist, who then repeats this inspiring story to others, the Elder was successful. And Cardinal continued to be a strong champion of Cree culture. In the same 2005 talk, he writes that:

> Throughout the eons of time preceding the arrival of the White man to our lands and territories, our peoples evolved, developed, maintained and sustained complex systems through which they continued the knowledge quest ... Many describe our systems of pursuing knowledge as "holistic" in the sense that our systems of knowledge did not isolate knowledge in a way, which separated the spiritual from the physical aspects of First Nation life.[25]

Using this concept of intergenerational and holistic search for knowledge changed my study of Cree and Métis lifewriting. Seeing autobiography as an Indigenous intellectual tradition allows me to move beyond colonization as a prism with which to examine Indigenous life and literature. I stopped applying a postcolonial paradigm to Indigenous life stories because our concepts begin long before the history of colonialism; I stopped relying on vocabulary like "resistance literature," "testimonio," and "witnessing," coined by autobiography studies, because while these terms are useful for certain conversations, they can also reinscribe an identity as colonized and leave us less able to engage with writing that is not overtly "resistant" or political.

I try to approach the neglected texts of this study using Cree paradigms to ask new questions: for example, instead of looking for agency in Edward Ahenakew's *Voices of the Plains Cree*, I wonder what Cree values he demonstrates; instead of examining subversive strategies in Joseph Dion's *My Tribe, the Crees*, I wonder how the author, a teacher for twenty-four years and a Status Cree activist for Métis rights, exhibits a nêhiyaw understanding of history, pedagogy and relationships. And when I come across Eleanor Brass's

I Walk in Two Worlds, I wonder how she, as a Cree intellectual, valued her obligation to pass on the knowledge to the next generation.[26] And key to all this inquiry is the question of how I, too, as someone in this subsequent generation, am implicated in this process.

While Cardinal articulates a Cree relationship to knowledge that is fundamentally different than conventional academic approaches, central to his approach are autobiographical questions. The questions that his Elder asks him ("who is it that you really are?") and Cardinal's subsequent meditation reveal his understanding of knowledge as intertwined with self-knowledge. This necessarily prods me to consider my own responsibilities to Cree knowledge and to generations before and after me.

It would be easy to lament the knowledge loss that I have witnessed in my family. While I relate the fact that I do not speak fluent Cree because I did not grow up near my mother's hometown, I know that many of my cousins struggle with Cree, even if they grew up around a Cree-speaking community with Elders nearby. And while our grandmother and her mother, our kôhkom and câpân, were accomplished medicinalists, none of their children or grandchildren has this training.

As I grew up on army and air force bases across Western Canada, we often visited family during the summer. (I have countless cousins.) But even when we were not nearby, my mother kept family central through storytelling, drawing on an archive that was highly autobiographical. To recite the name of each uncle and auntie is to remember a volume of stories told to me by my mother, about their childhoods, the families they married into, their children. Even though she never wrote any down, Mom was a remarkable storyteller, with incredible comic timing and turn of phrase, able to tell you and retell you these stories your whole life and then one day tell you one you had never heard before. Because this wasn't true of my Dad, I know much less about his side of the family. My paternal grandmother passed away before I was born, and I never knew three out of my Dad's four half-siblings. We did have regular visits with the families of my Dad's three younger siblings, and we all remember with great fondness our Auntie Lena. While I remember laughter, I don't remember stories of the past. Most of what I know about that side of the family is what Mom heard and shared with us.

In summers we would return to Saskatchewan and stop and visit in Saskatoon or P.A.—Prince Albert—on our way up to La Ronge. Sometimes we would go even farther and stay with kôhkom at the trapping cabin at Eight-and-a-Half, named for the distance it was from somewhere not obvious to me. I don't remember communication being a problem during the time I spent with kôhkom, but I never remember her speaking a word of English. I remember being beside her when she pulled out of the lake a large plastic bag where she kept food she wanted to keep cool, to get me margarine for bannock. At some point, I got tired and a little weak from breathing too much smoke around the fire, and she and my mother made a hammock or wêwêpison that I could rest upon. Animal hides hung on the clothesline and plants were strung from the ceiling to dry, the first step in the process by which kôhkom would make medicines. As a girl, Mom would deliver these to people who had asked kôhkom for help, but always on the sly as the practice was frowned upon by the priest. This isn't to say that kôhkom wasn't devout, for she regularly went to church, sent her children to First Communion, and practiced Catholicism rather than anything that we might recognize as Indigenous spirituality today. But when she cured a man from blindness, a fact undisputed by any of her children, she relied on a dream that helped her find the right medicine. When some people suggested that her medicines were voodoo, she would scoff with derision because she considered them to be talking out of ignorance. I felt a certain validation about this family story when I came across an essay by Cree language teacher and Elder Stan Cuthand, who recounted his early years in La Ronge as an Anglican minister. He cited kôhkom as one of the "medicine people in La Ronge who were well known for their ability to heal the sick. [She] and Mr. Jerrimiah McKenzie both have a wide reputation for their healing powers."[27]

When I went to visit her and my grandfather en route to Montreal to go to university, they were both well over eighty and living in a seniors' home. Out from her closet, kôhkom pulled out a bag of herbs she had collected and gave them to me, to make myself tea when I needed it. I've often wondered if she could tell that by the time I would arrive in my new city that I would fall sick with pneumonia. Regardless, the tea she gave me was comforting. The previous year had been difficult as my father had passed on, unexpectedly, at the age of fifty-one. When I saw a poster advertising a program that sent undergraduates to Quebec to work as English tutors in public high schools for a couple of hundred dollars a month, I recognized this to be a way to escape my family's grief and evening shifts as a waitress at the Oakridge White Spot.

While I had managed to enroll in English literature and Liberal Arts classes at Concordia's downtown campus and rent an apartment just the other side of Rue St. Catherine, I didn't have a bed or even a telephone when I was struck down. I lay on a thin foam mattress that I had brought with me and was overtaken by a dream that I remember vividly. I was aware that I was lying on the floor of my bachelor apartment and that I wanted a cup of tea but didn't have the strength to make it. Suddenly I saw a gigantic bird gliding above me, high in the sky, circling above me and making increasingly larger arcs until it was circling above the whole neighbourhood, the whole city, everywhere as far as it could see. I knew that this bird was looking for someone who knew me and would come and take care of me, but as far as it could fly, it could find no one.

After I recovered from pneumonia and came to love my studies and Montreal, I never was able to shake a certain sense of isolation and the sense that I was alone; I never saw any reflection of or reference to my community in any of my classes, which only served to reinforce my fear that "Indians" hadn't done anything worth studying and that Native people—the term I would use then—didn't go to university. If it weren't for my appearance, which causes people to ask me my ethnicity, I wouldn't ever have mentioned my Cree-Métis roots. It was years before I recognized that my understanding of the world as stories, linked together, to read closely or mull over, as well as my love for literature, are the result of my mother's continual storytelling that permeated my childhood and, I think, wired my brain.

In *Native Poetry in Canada*, Okanagan Syilx scholar Jeannette Armstrong grafts the history of the field onto her life story. In her introduction she uses a short autobiography to describe the series of epiphanies she had as she discovered Indigenous writers in contexts where Indigenous people are generally absent. It begins in 1965 when, from her reserve classroom, her cousin points to "the Indian guy who wrote a book."[28] She describes how she and her classmates "rushed to the window to look at him, awestruck ... The only published 'Indian' most of us had heard of then was Pauline Johnson."[29] She recalls her sense of pride when Chief Dan George visited her community in 1967 to read "Lament for Confederation," because he "sounded like us."[30] She felt a visceral thrill when Duke Redbird's poetry was able to "make it to radio,"[31] because in Redbird's work she recognized "the underlying 'Native' themes."[32] All of this leads up to her participation in the red-hot Native poetry scene of the 1980s, culminating in 1988, when "the International Feminist Book Fair in Montreal brought together over fifteen prominent Native women writers from Canada and the United States to comment on Native Writing."[33] She credits this event with the establishment of the En'owkin School of Writing in her territory, ushering in an "era of literary proliferation reinforcing an appreciation of Native cultural diversity."[34]

At this conference, Lee Maracle set off a storm of controversy when she asked non-Native writer Anne Cameron to abandon her practice of publishing Native stories.[35] Cameron argued that she was given permission to use the Nuu-chah-nulth stories on which her bestseller, *Daughters of Copper Woman*,[36] is based. In her contribution to *Language in Her Eye: Writing and Gender*,[37] Lee Maracle records many voices at that event:

> The truth is that a statement I made at the Third International Feminist Book Fair, objecting to the appropriation of our stories, has

nothing to do with censorship. "We are not monkey grunters in need of anyone to tell our stories." "We have a voice." "Don't buy books about us, buy books by us." And, "Move over."[38]

Embedded in these quotations is an assessment of the state of publishing at that time. In the late 1980s non-Indigenous authors like Cameron, W. P. Kinsella,[39] and Darlene Barry Quaife[40] were finding acclaim writing books from what they considered a Native perspective, while Native authors were having difficulty finding publishers. Criticisms by Indigenous intellectuals of appropriation of voice, or appropriation of stories, were dismissed as endorsements of censorship, limiting authors' rights to create a work using characters of any ethnicity or write about any topic they chose. By refusing to consider her critique to be censorship, Maracle is not engaging with the complaints of non-Indigenous authors. Instead, by using a montage of voices, she brings the focus back to Indigenous interests. Anyone familiar with Jeannette Armstrong, who is a cultural expert, carrying herself with authority and dignity, would understand the sense of outrage and insult that she expresses in the one quote, "We are not monkey grunters." Anyone familiar with Chrystos and her poetry knows the strength of her words and how she has endured. It is incredible that someone who speaks so clearly, even loudly, would have to say, "We have a voice." So obvious as to almost be redundant are the words of editor Viola Thomas, who points out that there is a difference between "books about us" and "books by us." The final phrase, "Move over," referring to the name of the paper Maracle delivered at this conference, evokes rhetoric of the Civil Rights movement. Maracle's phrase "Move over" not only demands a space for Indigenous authors but points out that those present with power need to relinquish some for change to occur.[41]

While I don't think I was present during these specific debates, I was, in fact, at the International Feminist Book Fair at the University of Montreal. I went as an undergraduate, about halfway through my BA. While I was familiar enough with French that I could follow along with casual conversations, this conference drew participants from around the world who spoke many different languages. We had to use earphones to listen to translations of scholarly papers, work that was already densely theoretical, and I almost fainted from the alienation.

At this point, I was enrolled in a Great Books program at Concordia University that focussed on the Western canon, and so the curriculum did not feature any Indigenous theorists or authors. While I was initially thrilled that I had moved to an exciting city, and was finally studying "important" writers, I was also facing a crisis of identity because I never recognized myself in almost anything I researched. By the time I wandered around the building in which the conference was held, the anxiety I was feeling was palpable as I tried to understand why I was there. I remember finding a payphone to see if my partner would join me, just so that I would be able to see a friendly face.

He joined me in time to attend an afternoon session of about a dozen poets, all Indigenous women from across North America who were giving readings of their work.[42] At the time I didn't know that any of these women were famous, except for Chrystos, because I had just finished reading *Not Vanishing.* She told us that her literary production was slowing down because she only wrote when she was unhappy, and this had changed for her in recent years. The emcee, I remember, was Alanis Obomsawin—and for some reason I can't recall, she asked Margo Kane to read for her. Jeannette Armstrong and Joy Harjo were there, although at the time I didn't know who they were. But I remember responding to each poem, and I chuckled afterwards when I recalled the poem by a Native American woman about how much her uncle loved to drink coffee.[43]

Being in this room, I felt elation and relief, having the comfort of a loved one with me, and the feeling that these poems were rescuing me from suffocation; I also felt a sense that I was "at home." For the first time in a university setting did I think, "Yes, my mother would be comfortable here." I am still grateful to those poets and the organizers of that session. It seemed to me, finally, that I could be both an academic and a Métis woman without contradiction.

On Thanksgiving weekend 2000, a few weeks before my mother died, I flew from British Columbia with my cousin Janet and her daughter Crystal to attend a family reunion in La Ronge. We had a memorial service for Uncle Dave, who had passed on the previous year. Not since Grandpa's funeral in 1991 and kôhkom's funeral in 1993 had I seen so many of us all together. I wandered about thinking of Mom, who at sixty was the baby of the family, and instead of taking pictures, I carried around a tape recorder and asked people to record messages that I could bring back for her. Younger cousins didn't have as much to say, just giving their names and sending on a "Hi there, Auntie Delphine." Her brother, Victor, shy and reserved, said hello in English and sent kind words. But when I came to a table with my oldest cousins, who were just a few years younger than my mom, they grabbed hold of the recorder and started teasing Mom about her admonishments to them when she had been their babysitter. Sitting with them were the Mackay girls, who had grown up next door and had been my mother's closest friends. They made a few jokes in Cree, translating quickly for me in English, while the table erupted in laughter.

Janet came over to tell me that cousin Leo and his wife Diane were looking for gumboots for her and Crystal, so that they could all go for the afternoon to the old trapping cabin at Eight-and-a-Half. I went instead to visit my cousin Peggy and Auntie Jane, spending the afternoon drinking tea with them, going through a giant garbage bag filled with old photographs. At some point I was handed a photo of my mother's first communion. The version my mother owned—and I grew up seeing—was taken in haste, with my Auntie Irene half cut-off and the younger children looking stern and uncomfortable. Generally, when Mom saw this particular photo, she would tell me about her childhood summers spent in convents, picking peas in their garden, being warned by the nuns of the dangers of sin. What galled her was the nuns' hypocrisy because she witnessed them on summer Saturday nights, drinking, smoking, dancing. But in this version the photo is well-staged; my mother and aunties in pretty white dresses, my Uncle Dave in a smart black suit, my mother, the youngest, looking relaxed, happy.

There were also a set of photographs taken when I was seven. We had stayed with Uncle George and Auntie Jane for what seemed to be months, and I had spent a lot of time following around my older cousins, Peggy and Sylvia. The day we had left, my parents had taken a handful of pictures of the two families, some with the cousins together with the dog, some with the adults and kids, all pictures I had grown up looking at. It surprised me to realize that Auntie Jane had a mirror set taken with a different camera at the same time. Similar but from slightly different positions. It wasn't until then that I realized that the shots were always incomplete. The photo never included the person who snapped the picture.

Fig. 7 The four youngest Patterson children at First Communion, c. 1948 (left to right): Francoise Delphina, David, Irene, and Vicky. Reder family photo.

All of this was a visual representation of the existence of multiple perspectives and the fact that each point of view has both a unique vantage point and a limitation. My first training in thinking about this began with family stories. From these I learned the shifting nature of any narrative based on who is telling the story, and when and in what context they are speaking from. Different versions don't necessarily change the facts of the story, but like the pictures, there is always going to be someone or something left out. This coincides with one of the most basic tenets of autobiography theory, articulated by Paul John Eakin in 1985, that autobiography cannot "offer a faithful and unmediated reconstruction of a historically verifiable past; instead, it expresses the play of the autobiographical act itself, in which the materials of the past are shaped by memory and imagination to serve the needs of present consciousness."[44] While Eakin was defending the genre from long-held criticism by historians on the unreliability and bias of autobiography, his definition accommodates, however unintentionally, a Cree epistemology. Cree scholar Neal McLeod insists in his 2005 dissertation that:

> The inclusion of Cree narrative interpretive structures does not mean we abandon the truth: rather, it means that we accept a more nuanced understanding of historical truth, a concept which is comfortable with more than one interpretation existing simultaneously.... nêhiyâwiwin [Creeness] involves a high degree of subjectivity and a stress on individual interpretation.[45]

This valuing of interpretation is different from Western ways of knowing, bolstered by institutions like universities, through accompanying curricula like literary histories, that produce and promote canonical and highly ideological interpretations. In Indigenous stories the listener gets to be the critic because only in the act of engagement will we learn anything.[46] A major focus in accounts, as we read or hear them, is to consider the teachings in the story, rather than fixate on the truth value. What matters more is what you learn from the stories you hear; how you understand the perspectives of others that are undoubtedly different than your own.

Nestled among Auntie Jane's pictures were two I asked to borrow and copy. One was a picture of the camp at Eight-and-a-Half, probably taken from a canoe out on the lake during the summer I had spent there around age seven. This was such a mystical place to me that it amazed me that a picture of it existed. The other was a picture I had never seen before, of my mother looking so young, with me not quite two years old, and my cousins Sylvia and Robbie with Auntie Jane's mom, Mrs. Sanderson, sitting on a rock in the sunshine.

Fig. 8 At the camp at Eight-and-a-Half, summer 1965. Left to right: Francoise Delphina Reder, Deanna Reder, Sylvia Patterson, Mrs. Amelia Sanderson, and Robbie Patterson. Reprinted with permission of the Patterson family.

At the family party that night, I pulled out family pictures that had been stored in my mother's old purse for my entire childhood. I had arranged them in an album one Christmas, just after she had moved into the hospital, and I wanted to show them here and find out what others the rest of the family had. The reaction wasn't exactly what I expected. People were incredulous, as though I had brought out a time machine. While some, like Auntie Jane, had piles of snaps mostly from the 70s, no one even remembered seeing these circa 1950s photos. Cousin Leo and Diane smiled when they saw our grand-father with another older man, Mr. Bird. They told me that their daughter Vanessa and John Bird's grandson had a newborn son of their own, and they marvelled that a photo existed with their grandson's two great-grandfathers standing together. My cousin Gerry Bell, who had such a pain-filled life from the time he was a teenager —when his mother, Auntie Bella, died—until his middle age, marvelled at the picture of him as a happy little kid of about five years of age, riding a tricycle over a patch of dirt. If you look closely you can see his feet spinning. Gerry's sister, Joanne, looked at the picture I had of her, about seven, crouched down next to my mom, then seventeen, as though she had seen a ghost: "I don't have any pictures of myself as a child," she told me.

Fig. 9 Joanne Bell (left) with Mom, c. 1958. Reder family photo.

We started talking about what we knew about the old times and the subject of medicine came up. Kôhkom was a well-known healer in her time, learning from her mother and the women before her, but not one of her ten children had her knowledge and training. Auntie Maureen, or maybe it was Auntie Janet, said that she remembered when one of her kids had a bad diaper rash and kôhkom had made a special salve. Somebody reminded us of how our aunties would find sap from trees to chew like store-bought gum. Leo said that he would go out and pick the leaves of a certain tree whenever he felt a cold coming on. Lillian reminded us about ratroot. And I told them about pee. When I was little and taking swimming lessons, I got this terrible rash on my toes. Mom told me that kôhkom would have me soak my feet in my own pee. Of course, I was distraught when Mom took me to the doctor's office. The nurse wanted a sample of my urine and I thought I knew what she had in mind.

Sharing these memories, we were comforted to know that while none of us knew what our grandmothers had known, it wasn't completely lost. We all remembered cures for different illnesses, different fragments of what was once a corpus of knowledge, fragments waiting to be collected together.

mâwaci nistam ohci ohcitaw piko ta-natohtaman êkwa ta-kiskisiyan.
kâ-ati-ispayik nawac mistahi kîkway ka-atoskâtên.
ohcitaw piko ta-mâtinamâkêyan anima kâ-kiskêyihtaman
kitâniskotâpânak ohci.

In the beginning you have the responsibility to listen and remember.
As time goes by your responsibilities increase.
You have to share what you know with the next generation.

Conclusion

So much of what it means to be Indigenous is under attack and prescribed by outside forces that tell us what we ought to look like and think and act and feel. That tell us how we ought to write or whether we even ought to—whether writing is our way. Whenever I hear our people repeat the saying that we come from an oral culture, I nod my head in respect for those story cycles I have heard retold while visiting together, for the musicians and poets who sing out their words in coffee houses or conferences, or for the teachings, songs, and addresses I've heard shared in longhouses or classrooms or in ceremony. But I also think of all the writing—all the unpublished or unread writing by our people—often dismissed by the publishing industry as not good enough, at least not good enough to release. I think about how we come from oral *and* literary cultures, even if this writing hasn't made it to the libraries or into school curriculum yet.

When I think about Chapter One, about the value of âcimisowin, of autobiography as an Indigenous intellectual tradition, I think about how engrained autobiographical practices are in our cultures, when we recognize the importance of declaring our position on the land on which we are situated, either as people of that territory or as uninvited guests on someone else's. Whether we are introducing ourselves by listing those relatives who have gone before us, or through the families to whom we belong, or by the connections we currently nurture, we emphasize the importance of our world view that is based on the interrelatedness of all things, wâhkôhtowin. And we see âcimisowin in forms beyond ceremony and verbal introductions, in "texts" that include writing, whether in book form, or in writing in the air as tweets or blogs. Furthermore, emphasizing our position we are emphasizing that knowledge is not objective but instead situated and grounded in the places where we stand.

In Chapter Two, as I remember about the âcimisowin of Maria Campbell, I think about the teachings she shares with us, that let us know that we can only understand our obligations if we understand how we are connected. The recognition of wâhkôhtowin brings an understanding of the work we must do. But I also struggle with the idea that a young author, on the verge of becoming one of the most important writers in the twentieth century, could bravely decide to write about a sexual assault that she suffered and in that moment of courage, in that desire to challenge and change society, that editors would have more control over her manuscript than she would, as evidenced by their actions to snip out a page and a half in direct opposition to her wishes.

In Chapter Three, I think about the wisdom shared with us by Edward Ahenakew. His expression of kihcêyihtamowin, of respect for people, wasn't just an act of protocol or politeness but an act of intellectual and emotional power. He modelled open-mindedness as a Cree value, uncowed by the racism and small thinking that he regularly witnessed and suffered. I offer the work on Ahenakew as an act of respect that I hope will help bring his work to full view, especially given how much his corpus has suffered from disrespectful and destructive editing practices.

In Chapter Four, I marvel at the ways in which Ahenakew's entire corpus exhibits âniskwâcimopicikêwin, an interrelatedness of texts and stories and land and ceremony. It will only be possible to understand the scope of this work once all his writings have been published, so that we can fully appreciate what nêhiyaw life was like in his era. Ahenakew knows our ways have been under attack. Sometimes we are caught in difficult dilemmas that, for the moment, we cannot solve. Sometimes we have had to bury the pipe and take other roads.

There is something so human in Edward Ahenakew's choice of the romance as a genre to imagine otherwise. The underlying question his heroes grapple with is: "what or who are they going to love and serve?" There is also a dark side to his description of his hero in *Black Hawk*. Allan Hawk looked like Ahenakew and lived like him—bookish with the ambition to become a doctor and serve his people—but Allan, likely because of his talents and charms and achievements and the fact that *Black Hawk* is fiction, is able to walk in society with all doors open to him, whereas, for Ahenakew, living in the actual world, many doors were slammed shut. Ahenakew carries the psychic burden of the Indigenous intellectual who knows how welcomed to any room we might be if only we were perfect; and because perfect, like Allan Hawk in his conversations with Helen, able to reason with any racist and change their minds and hearts on the spot.

In Chapter Five, even as I admire so much the accomplishments of Jim Brady, I rankle with the way he did not receive the intellectual opportunities that he ought to have had. I rankle at the lack of concern by authorities when he and Abbie Halkett went missing. But I also recognize that all the tellings and retellings that I heard as I grew up, about how kôhkom cured Abbie, about the ways that Jim and Abbie were lost, demonstrate the valuable, powerful ways that they continue to be named and remembered. And I intend this writing to be a contribution to ongoing efforts to celebrate their memory and their legacies.

When I think about Chapter Six and the lessons Harold Cardinal shares with us that he has learned from an Elder, I recognize that just as previous generations have passed kiskêyihtamowin, knowledge, to us, we might not be expected to understand in exactly the same way, but we are expected to pass on what we can to the next generations. I think about the question by the Elder: awîna mâka kiya—who is it that you really are? Even Harold Cardinal, a fluent Cree speaker, an intellectual, at an early point in his life didn't understand how to answer the question. I think about how I have been supported to understand who I am. And I think of my children, my grandchildren, and my great-grandchildren who, depending on how they live their lives and who they make families with, will have to ask themselves if they share nêhiyawi-itâpisinowin, a Cree worldview. Their answers will mostly depend on forces that I might have put into motion by the way I raised my children, by the fact that we lost my mother—their kôhkom—along with almost all of my aunts and uncles when they were small, and on how they come to understand themselves in relation to their Dad's family. Regardless, they and their children and grandchildren will always be much loved and through that love connected to me; they will always be my children, my grandchildren, my great-grandchildren, my relatives.

Through all of this work, I think about the fact that while we speak from specific positions, these shift and change as we grow and move and learn and age. We are hurtling through time and space, connected by these stories to those who have preceded us and to those who will come after us, but also to those we love and to where we once were—or perhaps it is clearer to say, who we once have been. While I was a young girl, my job was to listen and remember. As an adult and an academic, I have increased responsibilities. Family members can call you into a story and compel you to become involved. Authors themselves can call out to you to have you read their work, and then to look for more of their writing, and if so, this comes with obligations. This book is meant to fulfill some of them by remembering âcimisowina, and the missing and long missed people, stories, and perspectives held within.

Acknowledgements

My first words of thanks go to my mother, whose stories grounded me wherever I went, even though it took me a few years to realize how precious they were, and to my father, who urged me to get as much education as I could. While I wish they had the chance to know their grandchildren, I know they would be as grateful for them as I am.

I also thank my husband, Eric Davis, who has been for years both my strongest supporter and my first reader. He has always taken seriously my desire to return to school, even when it seemed implausible. Thanks also to my children, Sam, Eli, and Mischa, who had to suffer through several moves to deal with changing family circumstances, and then years of distraction as I focused on my studies and then this book. I hope this work resonates with you.

As for inspiration, I still remember being at the Ogamas Aboriginal Literary Festival at Brandon University in either 2008 or 2009 when I had the immense privilege to stand in a circle, visiting, with Louise Halfe, Gregory Scofield, Tomson Highway, and Neal McLeod, when everyone was speaking Cree. It was a transformational moment that emphasized to me the vitality of our writers and our language. And kinanâskomitin to the nêhiyawak and âpihtawikosisânak who have inspired this work. I remain ever grateful for the vision of the writers I have been privileged to study. I have so much respect and gratitude for James Settee, Edward Ahenakew, Harold Cardinal, James Brady, Absolom Halkett, and especially for Maria Campbell. All of your work will be cherished by future generations.

I remain thankful to the theorists who draw on our culture to transform scholarship. Thank you to Lorraine Brundige Mayer, Winona Wheeler, Tasha Beeds, Brenda Macdougall, Sherry Farrell-Racette, Warren Cariou, Neal McLeod, Emma LaRocque, Jesse Rae Archibald-Barber, Madeleine McIvor, Margaret Kovach, Shawn Wilson, and Keith and Linda Goulet. Much gratitude to the late Janice Acoose, whose work was so brave, and to the late Gregory Younging, who inspired us and left us with much to do. And kinanâskomitin to Arden Ogg from the Cree Literacy Network and to language expert Solomon Ratt.

Thank you to my research partners on The People and the Text, including Margery Fee, Daniel Heath Justice, Brendan Edwards, Rick Monture, Warren Cariou, and Rudy Reimer. We were able to do so much and I recognize there is still so much to do. Special recognition needs to go to the many students who worked on the archival material as part of The People and the Text, including Natalie Knight, Rachel Taylor, Alix Shield, Treena Chambers, Kimberley John, Lara Estlin, Alison Wick, Matthew Provost, Alexa Manuel, Jakob Knudsen, Patrick Canning, Sandie Dielissen, Maddie Reddon, Sarah Hedley, and Jessica Bound. Thank you for all your efforts. Thanks to the Social Sciences and Humanities Research Council for providing funding and for Simon Fraser University's grants facilitator, Beverly Neufeld, for her sage advice. Thank you also for the support by staff in the Department of Indigenous Studies, especially Shagufta Saddiq.

Thank you to Brendan Edwards whose work anticipated mine by several years. I am finally catching up. And thank you to Donald Smith, who has shared his knowledge with me from the moment we first met, generously paving the way for me but also for the next generation. And much gratitude to historian Peter Geller, who drew my attention to archives on James Settee and his dedication to ethical research. Thanks also to Skip Hambling who remembers going to England with the Association of Métis and Non-Status Indians of Saskatchewan (AMNSIS) in the early 1980s as if it were yesterday, and to Karon Schmon from the Gabriel Dumont Institute, who gave permission for us to reproduce a photograph that accompanied Skip's article about the event. Much appreciation to both the archives of the Province of Saskatchewan and to the Glenbow Museum Library and Archives. Thanks to those who have begun much-needed work on James Brady, including Paul Seesequasis, Sherry Farrell-Racette, Molly Swain, Eric MacPherson, and Michael Nest. Your work helps shine light on my own.

Special thanks to all my collaborators, all who have become trusted friends. First of all, to my supervisor, Margery Fee, thank-you for your work to open up the field of Indigenous literary studies and for your years of support. I hope we can continue to collaborate to complete all the projects we envision. Thank you to Linda Morra, who constantly guides me by her excellent example and her words of encouragement. Thank you to Sophie McCall, whose intelligence, energy, and kindness mark all her work. Her devotion to leveraging our roles as professors to create opportunities for students and Indigenous artists always challenges us to think creatively. It is an honour to work with her. Thank you to Michelle Coupal for her passion for the writing in our field and for our writers, for her value of excellence and ethics, and her grace under fire. Our original collaboration with partners Emalene A. Manual and Joanne Arnott was the epitome of excellent cooperation. Thank you to

Alix Shield, whose dedication to Indigenous research ethics is a model for all. Thank you to Michael Nest and Eric Bell for their comradery, steadfast commitment, and talent to continue to research a sensitive and complex story.

Much respect and love for the late Jo-Ann Episkenew and the late Renate Eigenbrod, who shared not just their ideas and mentorship but also their friendship. Likewise, special thanks to valued colleagues whose work informs and inspires mine: Niigaan Sinclair, Sophie McCall, June Scudeler, Jeannette Armstrong, Keavy Martin, Sam McKegney, Warren Cariou, Rick Monture, Kristina Bidwell, Sarah Henzi, Élise Couture-Grondin, Patrizia Zanella.

Thank you and much respect to my original supervisory committee, Margery Fee, Jo-ann Archibald, and Laura Moss. It is my work with them all those years ago that set the foundation for this book. It was a privilege to work with them. And thank you so much to all the editors of this book, including those who read early drafts, like Rachel Taylor, Margery Fee, Maddie Reddon, Linda Morra, Eric Davis, Eli Reder-Davis, Suzanne Mathieson-Bates, Julie Rak; thanks also to the Wilfrid Laurier University Press team: Lisa Quinn, Siobhan McMenemy, Murray Tong, Clare Hitchens, and copy editor Alicia Hibbert. A special thanks to the anonymous reviewers whose feedback made me realize what ideas needed to be more clearly expressed, helping this become a stronger book.

Special thanks to my family, especially the older generation. It is the stories of Victor Patterson, Irene Tomkins, Jane Patterson, and Frank Tomkins that have corroborated the stories that I heard from my mother. Thanks also to my brother, Bradley Reder, and our many cousins who have also shared thoughts and stories, especially Peggy Hunt, Lillian Sanderson, and Eric Bell. Thanks to cousin Joanne Bell for keeping our great-grandmother's prayerbooks safe and for Stephen Bagwell for sharing the scans with me. Thanks to Keltie Patterson who as a teenager appreciated the value of the history of our grandparents and arranged to video an interview of our grandfather, and to Auntie Maureen for making me a copy.

Finally, I am so grateful to the artist George Littlechild for his beautiful painting that graces the cover of this book. He listened to a foundational story in my family, about how kôhkum cured a man from blindness, and translated the story into an image that celebrates kôhkum's power, intelligence, and beauty.

Notes

Note to Cree Glossary of Terms

1 The editorial approach of this book to Cree language usage has been articulated by Tasha Beeds in her essay, "Rethinking Edward Ahenakew's Intellectual Legacy": "Although many Indigenous scholars demarcate a line between 'nêhiyaw' and 'Métis,' I include both together (in keeping with a teaching from Maria [Campbell] in order to recognize the fluid kinship lines and to recognize their shared worldview.... When I use the term 'nêhiyawak,' I am referring to those who see the world through nêhiyawi-itâpisiniwin (Cree way of seeing / worldview)." Beeds, "Intellectual Legacy," 119–31. The word for Cree worldview, "nêhiyawi-itâpisiniwin" is alternately spelled in Standard Roman Orthography or SRO as "nêhiyawi-itâpisinowin."

Notes to Introduction

1 Wolfart, "Cree Literature," 243–47.
2 Because Cree spelling is not fully standardized, many of the sources I have relied upon throughout my research vary their spelling. When I quote directly I almost always use the exact spelling of the words as written by their authors but when I refer to these concepts, I rely on Standard Roman Orthography, or SRO, as used in the Plains Cree dictionary (https://itwewina.altlab.app/); this is a reliable source, accessible to readers. Also, while the convention is to italicize *foreign* words, I avoid italicizing Cree words.
3 Wolfart, "Cree Literature," 246.
4 Wolfart, 246.
5 Brundige, "Tanisi," 37.
6 See Harding, *Feminist Standpoint Theory Reader*.
7 Crasnow, "Contemporary Standpoint Theory," 189.
8 Haraway, *Simians, Cyborgs, and Women*, 190.
9 Cariou, *Lake of the Prairies*, 11.
10 Cariou, 5.
11 See also Cree education theorist Margaret Kovach's chapter "Situating Self, Culture, and Purpose in Indigenous Inquiry" in Kovach, *Indigenous Methodologies*, 109–20.
12 See Blaeser, "Native Literature," 51–62; Womack, *Red on Red*.
13 LaRocque, "Preface," xxvi.
14 In keeping with the rules of house style, I preserve the spelling of the author within the quote but for the discussion outside of this, I revert to the form of the word that is present in Standard Roman Orthography, or SRO. So LaRocque uses the spelling of "Wisakehcha," and when I quote her, I do so as well. However, when I refer to the Cree trickster, I use the SRO version, which is wîsahkêcâhk, acknowledging that the English name is commonly spelled as Wisahkecahk.

15   LaRocque, "Preface," xv.

16   For LaRocque see Chapter One for a fuller discussion of the autobiographical aspects
     to her Preface; for Highway see McKegney, *Magic Weapons*; for Halfe see Halfe, "Key-
     note Address," 65–74 and Neuhaus, "Reading the Prairies Relationally," who argues
     that *The Crooked Good* is âcimisowin.

17   Minde, *Kwayask ê-kî-pê=kiskinowâpahtihicik*, xv.

18   Many Cree speakers retain the spelling for terms that they were taught; I respect that
     in the title of her 2021 lecture Campbell spells the Cree word for "my relations" as
     "ni'wahkomakanak"; for those more familiar with the spelling of the word in Standard
     Roman Orthography (SRO), I include it as "niwâhkômâkanak." Campbell, "Ni'wah-
     komakanak: All My Relations."

19   See Simpson, "Indigenous Resurgence," 20. Simpson values what she calls "grounded
     normativity"; she quotes Dene scholar Glen Coulthard (*Red Skin, White Masks*, 60)
     who defines it as "the system of ethics that are continuously generated by a rela-
     tionship with a particular place, with land, through the Indigenous processes and
     knowledges that make up Indigenous life." For Simpson ("Indigenous Resurgence," 22),
     grounded normativity needs to be central in order for decolonization to be possible.

20   Sometimes Frank's father was referred to as Peter Tomkins Junior to differentiate him
     from his father Peter Tomkins Senior, who had been a prisoner of war at Batoche.

21   The accomplishments of Norris and Brady are the subject of Dobbin, *The One-and-
     a-Half Men*.

22   See records in Tomkins personal archive, in the possession of the author. See also
     the entry on Frank Tomkins in *The Virtual Museum of Métis History and Culture*:
     https://www.metismuseum.ca/resource.php/03369. Note that the online resource
     lists the photo of Tomkins from the late 1970s when in fact it was from the same
     trip discussed by Skip Hambling, as part of the Association of Métis and Non Status
     Indians of Saskatchewan in 1981.

23   Hambling, "Constitutional Update," 8–10.

24   A detail shared with me in conversation with Skip Hambling.

25   See *Cree Code Talker*, about Charles "Checker" Tomkins, and featuring Frank Tom-
     kins, directed by Alexandra Lazorowich for the National Screen Institute Aboriginal
     Documentary in association with APTN in 2015.

26   In a point that I have only ever heard from Frank Tomkins, Cree was not actually
     an ideal language to use in a conflict with Germany because there were German
     missionaries who had learned Cree in their work in North America. It is for this
     reason, according to Frank, that the U.S. then switched to different Native American
     communities whose languages were more obscure than Cree.

27   I should note that there is one exception that I know of: my cousin Leo Patterson's
     wife, Diane, was raised with Michif.

28   Thanks to Anishinaabe scholar, professor, and journalist, Niigaanwewidam Sinclair
     who pressed this point to me in a conversation in 2017.

29   See Lutz, *Contemporary Challenges*, 42 for Maria Campbell's discussion with German
     scholar Hartmut Lutz about how "a whole section was taken out of the book that was
     really important, and I had insisted it stay there."

30   As part of work with The People and the Text, Yurok and Diné scholar Natalie Knight,
     at the time a doctoral student, and Iñupiaq editor Rachel Taylor, an undergraduate
     student, both at Simon Fraser University, carefully transcribed the handwritten manu-
     script. Brendan F. R. Edwards generously shared a portion of the manuscript that he
     had transcribed earlier, which they proofread and continued.

31 While typically unpublished manuscripts are enclosed in quotation marks, in this case I italicize the work that would have been published as *Old Keyam*, to distinguish it from the second half of the 1973 manuscript *Voices of the Plains Cree*, called "Old Keyam".

32 See Nest with Reder and Bell, *Cold Case North*.

33 Harold Cardinal first came to prominence in Canada in 1969 with the publication of *The Unjust Society*, written when he was a 23 year old law student.

34 See Cardinal, "Einew Kis-Kee-Tum-Awin." While I heard the talk at the University of British Columbia First Nation's House of Learning in March 2005, Dr. Cardinal composed a similar version of the talk for the AFN Special Chief's Assembly at the Renaissance Vancouver Hotel Harbourside on March 29, 2005. Cardinal gave a copy of this script to UBC and in it, he spells the question as "Awina Maga Kiya" rather than using SRO.

35 LaBoucane-Benson, et al., *Trauma*, 72.

Notes to Chapter One

1 Sections of this chapter were published as "Writing Autobiographically," 153–69, in the 2010 anthology edited by LaRocque, DePasquale, and Eigenbrod.

2 Johnson (Tekahionwake), "Song My Paddle Sings," 31–32.

3 There has been ample scholarship, especially in the United States, on the settler pretending to be "Indian" as a potent colonial fantasy. See Francis, *The Imaginary Indian*; Deloria, *Playing Indian*; Huhndorf, *Going Native*; and Young and Brunk, *Cultural Appropriation*.

4 Petrone, *First People*.

5 For example, at Poundmaker's 1885 trial the Cree leader testifies:

> I am not guilty ... When my people and the whites met in battle, I saved the Queen's men. I took the firearms from my following and gave them up at Battleford. Everything I could do was to prevent bloodshed.... You did not catch me. I gave myself up. You have me because I wanted peace. I cannot help myself, but I am still a man.

As noted in the entry by Bill Waiser in Hallowell, *Oxford Companion to Canadian History*, Poundmaker was found guilty of treason-felony and sentenced to three years in Stony Mountain Penitentiary. He was released after the first year and died shortly thereafter. On 23 May 2019 Prime Minister Justin Trudeau released a statement exonerating Poundmaker.

6 For example, in 1633 Montagnais chief Capitanal prefaces his arguments with a French explorer by describing himself as "bewildered; I have never had any instruction; my father left me very young" (as cited in Petrone, *First Voices*, 5); in 1786 the Mohawk chief, Joseph Brant, begins a letter: "I was, Sir, born of Indian parents, and lived while a child among those whom you are pleased to call savages"(36); see also Joe, *Song of Rita Joe*, as cited in *First Voices*, 191–93.

7 The ethnonym for Ojibway is Anishinaabe. Alternate spellings of Ojibway that are in more contemporary use are Ojibwa and Ojibwe. Two common spellings of Anishinaabe are Anishnabe and Anishnawbe.

8 Petrone, *First Voices*, 77.

9 Petrone, 106–7.

10 Petrone, *Native Literature*, 70.

11 Krupat and Swann, *I Tell You Now*.

12   Krupat and Swann, *I Tell You Now*, 5, quoted in Petrone, *Native Literature*, 201.

13   See Woods O'Brien, *Plains Indian Autobiographies*; Brumble III, *American Indian Autobiography*; Bataille and Sands, *American Indian Women*; Wong, *Sending my Heart*; Krupat, *Those Who Come After*.

14   Krupat, *For Those Who Come After*, 29, 31.

15   Krupat, 29, 21.

16   Krupat, 29.

17   Krupat, 30.

18   Petrone, *Native Literature*, 70.

19   When Krupat and Swann reissued *I Tell You Now: Autobiographical Essays by Native American Writers* in 2005, they removed the reference to writing autobiographically as "repugnant"; instead the newest version says: "Although tribal nations, like people the world over, kept material as well as mental records of collective and personal experience, the notion of telling the whole of any one individual's life or taking merely personal experience as of particular significance was, in the most literal way, foreign" (ix).

20   Petrone, *Native Literature*, 21; 12.

21   Walker, *Indian Nation*, 16.

22   For further discussion of Copway see Reder, "Indigenous Autobiography," 170–90; John Bird charts the historiography of the approaches to Copway from Donald Smith to Cheryl Walker, Bernd Peyer, and Cathy Rex in Bird, "'Stranger in a Strange Land.'"

23   Petrone, *First Voices*, 70 (my emphasis).

24   In 1988 Sneja Gunew noted the same sense of low expectations for writing by immigrant women in Australia, writers who were expected to document their life stories without literary flourish or avant-garde literary techniques. See Gunew, "Authenticity," 81–97.

25   Krupat, *For Those Who Come After*, 31, 5.

26   For a fuller discussion of the ways that Krupat's assumptions about writing reductively prescribes how an Indigenous person must therefore identify see Deanna Reder, "Native American Autobiography," 35–63.

27   This notion of binary opposition between oral Indigenous cultures and literate Western ones has been critiqued by Indigenous literary nationalists. Scholars such as Craig S. Womack, Daniel Heath Justice, Christopher B. Teuton, and Robert Warrior oppose the notion that writing is foreign to Native American people and assert that there exists a large archive of Indigenous work created along the spectrum from orality to literacy that is worthy of study. Womack, who is Creek and Cherokee, asserts that "Native people have been on the continent at least thirty thousand years ... For much of this time period, we have had literatures." Womack, *Red on Red*, 7. Justice, who is Cherokee, writes that "Indigenous peoples have always communicated ideas, stories, dreams, visions, and concepts with one another and with the other-than-human world, in whatever media have been most convenient and meaningful at the time." Justice, *Why Indigenous Literatures Matter*, 21–22. Teuton, also Cherokee, argues that "Sequoyah did not create or invent the Cherokee syllabary ... [but instead developed it] from a much older language" Teuton, *Deep Waters*, 3. And Warrior, who is Osage, insists that nineteenth-century Indigenous nonfiction—including autobiography—is a valuable part of a politically engaged and yet neglected intellectual inheritance; he emphasizes that it is "the oldest and most robust type of modern writing that Native people in North America have produced as they have sought literate means by which to engage themselves and others in a discourse on the possibilities of a Native future." Warrior, *The People and the Word*, xx. See also Gloria Elizabeth Chacón's discussion

of "the interconnectedness between ancient scripts, performances, provenance, narratives, and their blending with contemporary literature ... " Chacón, *Indigenous Cosmolectics*.

29   See Sarris, *Keeping Slug Woman Alive*; Womack, *Red on Red*; and DiNova, *Spiraling Webs of Relation*.

30   Portillo, *Sovereign Stories*, 4.

31   See Mann, "The Great Law of Peace," 329–337. Mann argues that Native Americans, and the Haudenosaunee and Indigenous peoples of the Northeast of America in particular, enjoyed a higher level of personal autonomy than Europeans.

32   See Brotherston, *Image of the New World*.

33   Shea, "Prehistory," 25–46 as cited in Graham and Lucero, "Lifewriting," 121–135.

34   Pequot writer William Apess (1798–1839) released his autobiography, *A Son of the Forest*, in 1829; Zitkála-Šá (1876–1938), also known as Gertrude Simmons Bonnin, was a Yankton Dakota writer whose several books were released early in the twentieth century and were instantly popular.

35   Graham and Lucero, "Lifewriting," 123.

36   Another example to support the idea that Krupat's ideas continue to hold sway is the 2008 article by Kathleen McHugh, "James Luna," 429–60. McHugh discusses a performance art piece that exists in video featuring performance artist and Luiseño tribe member James Luna, filmed by Isaac Artenstein. Titled *The History of the Luiseño People* the videoed performance is a series of clips of Luna involved in actions associated with corrosive stereotypes of the "drunken Indian." The point of this uncomfortable work, McHugh states is to "embody and enact the fundamental problems of history and self-representation confronting Native people." Yet McHugh demonstrates and perpetuates the problems she examines. She assesses the oral, collaborative, and autobiographical features of the video, and attributes them, not as recognizable elements typical in performance art, but rather as evidence that autobiography is alien to Indigenous people: she quotes Krupat to say that "Indian autobiographies are not a traditional form among Native peoples but the consequences of contact with white invader-settlers and the product of a limited collaboration with them" (xi). McHugh concludes that the collaboration of Luna and Artenstein can be attributed to the fact that "[d]ue to the realities of colonial history and conquest and the oral character of Native American culture, most Native American autobiographies were collaborative ... " in McHugh, "James Luna," 432.

37   Angel, *Preserving the Sacred*, 6–7.

38   Petrone, *First Voices*, 13.

39   Copway is identifying the Trent River in Ontario; in contemporary contexts, when someone discusses "the River Trent" they are likely referencing the river with this name in England.

40   Petrone, *First Voices*, 13.

41   Petrone, 13–14.

42   Doerfler, Stark, and Sinclair, *Centering Anishinaabeg Studies*, 397–98.

43   Absolon, *Kaandossiwin*, 13.

44   For example, in *Living on the Edge: Nuu-Chah-Nulth History from an Ahousaht Chief's Perspective*, Chief Earl Maquinna George integrates his voice into his people's history. He writes:

> I believe it is important to understand the Nuu-Chah-Nulth people and their relationship to the land and sea. This is my objective for this book. In particular, I will take you on an exploration of the history and environment of my home territory in Clayoquot Sound, and impart my feelings about growing up and surviving there

from my own experiences and perspectives. (14)

For George, not only is his story an integral part of the story of his people and his territory but, in keeping with Nuu-Chah-Nulth tradition, so is his name. He is the descendant of Chief Maquinna, a powerful leader in the late 1700s who was made famous in a captivity tale, *White Slaves of the Nootka: John R. Jewitt's Narrative of Capture and Confinement at Nootka*, written by Englishman John R. Jewitt and first published in. George is also the descendant of another Maquinna, born around 1835, who in 1896 dictated a letter to the editor of the *Victoria Daily Colonist* in defense of the potlatch, which had been made illegal by the Indian Act. The letter writer argues that the potlatch is similar to the white man's banking system. He begins his letter:

> My name is Maquinna! I am the chief of the Nootkas and other tribes. My great-grandfather was also called Maquinna. He was the first chief in the country who saw white men. That is more than one hundred years ago. He was kind to the white men and gave them land to build and live on. By and bye more white men came and ill treated our people and kidnapped them and carried them away on their vessels, and then the Nootkas became bad and retaliated and killed some white people. But that is a long time ago. I have always been kind to the white men. (letter to the editor, *Victoria Daily Colonist*, 1896; as cited in Petrone, *First Voices*, 69)

Just like his descendant after him, Maquinna interweaves the story of his people with his own.

45   LaRocque, "Preface," xv–xxx.

46   LaRocque, xxi.

47   See also Jo-ann Archibald, who in her 1997 PhD dissertation "Coyote Learns to Make a Storybasket: The Place of First Nations Stories in Education," explains that when she began her research with her Elders, she would introduce herself by telling them where and which family she comes from: "Identifying one in relation to place and family is part of knowing how one fits within the collective or larger cultural group, a wholistic knowing. Even though this practice may extend to other cultures, I include it here to show that it was and is important in Stó:lō contexts" (99, 7n). This work was particularly significant because it came after a century of the suppression of the Halq'eméylem language and Stó:lō people. While Archibald grew up listening to stories, she clarifies that she did not benefit, as a child, from her nation's cultural richness: "I did not hear traditional stories being told when I was a child; however I heard many life experience stories" (96).

48   Jennifer S.H. Brown, in "James Settee and his Cree Tradition: An Indian Camp at the Mouth of Nelson River Hudsons Bay" traces down the varying birthdates for Settee and states that there "is good reason to place his birthdate somewhere between 1809 and 1812" (36).

49   Bidwell, "Cree Literature in Saskatchewan," 5.

50   Bidwell, 8.

51   Special thanks to Research Assistants Kimberley John and Treena Chambers who transcribed and proofread Settee's handwriting, as part of their work for The People and the Text, in collaboration with historian Peter Geller.

52   Copway, "Life," 9.

53   Copway, 32–33.

54   Copway, 53.

55   Settee, "Settee's Life," 1.

56   Settee, 1.

57 Settee, 2.

58 Settee, 5.

59 Bell, "Gramophone," 9.

60 Bell, 7.

61 Bell, 9.

62 James Settee's conversation with Robert Bell can be found in Bell, Robert Bell Fonds, MG 29 B15 Vol. 54 in the National Archives of Canada.

63 Stevenson, "Calling Badger," 24.

Notes to Chapter Two

1 I ought to have recognized that some of my cousins attended residential school, which could have been an indication, but at the time the school was also referred to as an orphanage. Since their mom passed away at a young age, that seemed to explain to me why they went away to school.

2 1985 is when Bill C-31 came into effect. Status Indian women who marry non-Status men no longer lose their status, but a series of complicated rules concerning the status of their children and grandchildren have introduced their own inequalities.

3 See Silman, *Enough is Enough*. Upon the passing of Bill C-31 over 100,000 people regained their Status; however, the application process was difficult and disadvantaged poor women and their children. See Bob Joseph, *21 Things*, 19–23.

4 Innes, *Elder Brother*, 80.

5 Innes, 89.

6 While Howard Adams (*Prison of Grass, Canada from the Native Point of View*) and others have suggested that Halfbreed was a term used by Anglophones while Métis was used by Francophones, I did not see this distinction in my childhood.

7 That being said, my cousin Janet tells me she remembers that kôhkom knew how to jig. And my Status Cree Uncle Edmond, married to my Auntie Bella, was a champion fiddler.

8 Macdougall, "Wahkootowin," 434.

9 Giraud, *The Metis*.

10 Macdougall, "Wahkootowin," 436.

11 Macdougall, 444.

12 Sylvia Van Kirk (*Many Tender Ties: Women in Fur-trade Society, 1670–1870*) is rightly credited as the first to look at the role of Métis women in Canada's fur trade, even though she replicates the stereotypes of Indigenous women found in the written record. Jean Barman notes her focus on women who married officers in the fur trade in Barman, *On the Cusp*, 211. Sarah Carter (*Aboriginal People and Colonizers of Western Canada to 1900*) begins a new era when she argues that First Nations' trading routes prior to European contact predetermined the position of forts. Her emphasis on Indigenous interpretations of European settlement resonates in Macdougall's work.

13 Many family names have a variety of spelling in the archives; for example, Meraste is also spelled as Merastee, Merasté, Mirasty, Merasty.

14 See Maria Campbell's "Jacob," published as part of *Stories of the Road Allowance People* to consider the damage done when this knowledge is lost.

15 Beeds, "Intellectual Legacy," 119.

16 Episkenew, "Socially Responsible Criticism, 60.

17 Episkenew, 68.13.

18 Campbell, *Halfbreed*, 14–15.
19 Campbell, 16.
20 Campbell, 22.
21 For a discussion of the changing Canadian definition of who was eligible to be enrolled as a Status Indian at the time of Confederation, see Lawrence, "Gender," 3–31.
22 Campbell, *Halfbreed*, 18.
23 Campbell, 22.
24 Campbell, 26.
25 Campbell, 27.
26 Campbell, 43.
27 Campbell, 61.
28 Campbell, 61.
29 Sharing food was central to Indigenous cultures generally, and Cree and Métis culture as well—in *Tales of an Empty Cabin*, Grey Owl refers to sharing food as part of "the rigid creed of backwoods hospitality" (49).
30 Williams, *The Pass System*.
31 In *"Real" Indians and Others*, Bonita Lawrence deconstructs the common association of Indian authenticity with Indian status and membership on a rural reserve, and the parallel discounting of urban Indians as "inauthentic" (135).
32 For further discussion on racial/spatial segregation, see Razack, "Gendered Racial Violence," 121–56.
33 Campbell, *Halfbreed*, 11.
34 McLeod, "Exploring," 22.
35 McLeod, 20–21.
36 Campbell, *Halfbreed*, 47.
37 Campbell, 51.
38 Campbell, 52.
39 Campbell, 9. See also Dumont, *Good Brown Girl*.
40 Brundige, "Tanisi," 82–125.
41 Brundige, 116.
42 McLeod, "Exploring," 22.
43 Campbell, *Halfbreed*, 16.
44 Campbell, 11.
45 Campbell, 22.
46 Campbell, 52.
47 Campbell, 41.
48 Campbell, 115. This was most likely a 1940 Hollywood film directed by Cecil B. DeMille called *North West Mounted Police* and starring Gary Cooper. It is listed in a 1978 book, *The Fifty Worst Films of All Time*, by Harry Medved.
49 Campbell, 115.
50 Campbell, 11.
51 Campbell, 36.
52 Campbell, 163.
53 Campbell, 159.
54 Campbell, 159.
55 Campbell, 164.
56 Campbell, 180.
57 Campbell, 11.
58 In order to get land under the scrip system, Métis people would literally be divided. As Pamela Sing explains in a 2006 article in *Studies in Canadian Literature*:

When the Hudson's Bay Company sold Rupert's Land to the Canadian government, the latter signed two types of treaties with the Aboriginals who, in exchange, agreed to extinguish their property rights. The First Nations received collective treaties in the form of reserves, whereas the Métis had to apply for individual "scrips," certificates for either land or for money with which to purchase land. Several factors contributed, however, to the sale of such scrips for derisorily low sums and ultimately, to the loss of territory ... first, that the only eligible lands were those that had been surveyed, and that these were often not only found at a distance from those already occupied by the Métis, but also in scattered areas, so that families and communities would have to separate in order to take possession of a property; and second, the fact that several Métis, poverty-stricken, thought it more profitable to sell their scrips for immediate cash. ("Intersections of Memory," 112–13).

59 Brundige, "Tanisi," 124.
60 For a discussion of the value of autonomy and self-sufficiency in Cree culture, see LaBoucane-Benson et al., *Trauma*, 85–86.
61 LaBoucane-Benson et al., 85–86.
62 Campbell, *Halfbreed*, 76.
63 Campbell, 189.
64 Campbell, 2.
65 Campbell, 2.
66 Campbell, 189.
67 Rape survivors still face this silencing from police; see Doolittle, "The Unfounded Effect."
68 See Shield, "Kwaskastahsowin."
69 Campbell's publisher, McClelland & Stewart, suspected that the book would be successful, but never anticipated that the initial print run of 4500 copies would immediately sell out. They ordered an additional 4000, then another 2500, and struggled in that first year of publication to keep up with demand. Professors from across Canada lobbied for a paperback edition to teach in their classes. Universities at that time had little, if any, Indigenous content, and certainly nothing from a Métis perspective. For more details see Reder and Shield, "Recovering," 13–25.
70 Lutz, *Contemporary Challenges*, 47.
71 Both Canadianist Jennifer Andrews and Black literary studies scholar David Chariandy have shared with me their attempts as graduate students in the 1990s to find the missing passage without success.
72 Alix Shield uses Maria Campbell's spelling, kwaskastahsowin; in Standard Roman Orthography it is spelled as kwayaskwastâsowin.

Notes to Chapter Three

1 While now substantially revised, a flawed version of this chapter, limited by its use of an unreliable source, has been published. See Reder, "Understanding Cree Protocol," 50–64.
2 McLeod, "Cree Narrative Memory," 43.
3 Edward Ahenakew, "The Story of the Rev. Canon Edward Ahenakew," 1. Unpublished 14-page handwritten document as part of the Edward Ahenakew Papers in Saskatchewan Archives Board, Regina.
4 Edward Ahenakew, "Genealogical Sketch of My Family," 2.

5 Should any reader be tempted to differentiate between Indigenous and non-Indigenous autobiography, to suggest that Indigenous identity is communal whereas non-Indigenous (Western) identity is autonomous, please see Reder, "Native American Autobiography," where I discuss the words of autobiography theorist Paul John Eakin, who argues that no one is autonomous and "all identity is relational," "[a]ll selfhood ... is relational despite differences that fall out along gender lines." Eakin, "Relational," 64, 67.

6 In SRO "keyam" is spelled as "kiyâm".

7 Ahenakew, *Old Keyam*, 11; in Buck's version she edits it to say: "If we listen to what he has to say, perhaps we may understand those like him who know not what to do and, in disguising their bewilderment and their hurt, seem not to care" (52).

8 See David R. Miller, on Ahenakew, especially on publishing history. Miller, "Edward Ahenakew's Tutelage," 249–72.

9 I draw on archival material from fonds that are largely unpublished and inaccessible to the public, which, due to their nature, will not be found in the Bibliography, but will be referred to in notes and in-text. See Province of Saskatchewan archive file R_874.1_I.6a, p. 1. See also the beginning of the 1995 edition of Edward Ahenakew's *Voices of the Plains Cree*, ed Ruth M. Buck (Regina, SK: Canadian Plains Research Center, 1995) where there is a word of thanks to Ruth M. Buck by Christine (Willy) Hodgson, identified as the "daughter of Agnes Ahenakew Pratt and niece of Dr. Canon Edward Ahenakew." The footnote states: "The Ahenakew and Matheson families have experienced more than a century of friendship. Ruth Matheson Buck's generosity of spirit fired her efforts to reach for the dream of my uncle, Edward Ahenakew—the writing and publication of stories he heard in the 'voices' of the Plains Cree" (viii).

10 *Voices of the Plains Cree* was subsequently reissued in 1995 by the Canadian Plains Research Center with annotations and a new sixteen-page preface by Stan Cuthand. See Cuthand, "Preface," vii–xx.

11 Ahenakew's 1920 Address from archival sources, 5.

12 From archival sources, page 27 of Duncan Campbell Scott's, "the Indians and the Great War," published as part of the 1919 Annual Report of the Department of Indian Affairs.

13 Edward Ahenakew, "Old Keyam," 101.

14 See most of chapter XIII of an unpublished manuscript from archival sources, *Old Keyam*, by Edward Ahenakew; Ruth M. Buck left this passage out and instead ends reference to the League at the end of chapter seven with the statement: "For too long, we might have deserved—all of us together—the name 'Keyam'" (Buck, *Voices of the Plains Cree*, 85).

15 On the book jacket of the 1995 edition of *Voices of the Plains Cree* (Buck), Old Keyam is described as follows: "a fictional character, semi-autobiographical, he is very much the voice of Edward Ahenakew, telling of life on the reservations in the new white world of the early twentieth century." Others, like Cree literary critic Neal McLeod, considered Old Keyam to be "the semi-autobiographical voice of Edward Ahenakew" (McLeod, "Exploring," 147).

16 Ruth Buck writes that "the manuscript, in fact, represented a painful and even hazardous process of thought for Ahenakew *and it was never finished*" (emphasis added) (Buck, *Voices*, 14); for the purposes of this chapter I have omitted the second half of the line, in order to discuss it later. It is difficult to believe that Ahenakew could have submitted the manuscript to other publishers if in fact it was not completed, and given that an almost complete copy exists in the archive.

17 Buck, Introduction, xviii.

18 Buck, 13–14.

19 Ahenakew, *Old Keyam*, 3–4.

20 In Ahenakew's *Old Keyam*, 11; in Buck's version she edits it to say: "Still, he makes the effort to look also to the future" (52).

21 Stevenson (Wheeler), "Decolonizing," 180; see also Maria Campbell, "Kiasyno Akuâ Nehiawatsowin: Old Man and Cree Life Ways," unpublished manuscript in the possession of Wheeler.

22 The SRO for "napewatsowin," or man ways, is nâpêwatisowin, which means man ways, instructions on the way a man conducts himself, on how to be a man.

23 Wheeler, "Decolonizing," 183.

24 Thanks especially to Rachel Taylor (Iñupiaq), Natalie Knight (Dené and Yurok), Treena Chambers (Métis), Kimberley John (Sechelt), Marisol Cruz, and Patrick Canning (Heiltsuk) for completing the bulk of transcribing but also the help of other Research Assistants for The People and the Text including settler scholars Sandie Dielissen, Ali Wick, Lara Estlin, Sarah Hedley, Dani Randle, Jessica Bound, among many more.

25 Buck, *Voices*, 98.

26 Ahenakew, *Old Keyam*, between 107 and 108 is a ten-page essay titled "Old Keyam on Boarding Schools. The passages I discuss are on page 4 of that insert.

27 Buck, *Voices*, 90.

28 Buck, 90.

29 Ahenakew, *Old Keyam*, between 107 and 108 is a ten-page essay titled "Old Keyam on Boarding Schools." This passage comes from page 4 and 5 of that insert.

30 Buck, *Voices*, 90.

31 From archival sources, Spence and Ahenakew were photographed together with students at a Saskatchewan Lay Reader's School in 1954 and worked together again at an Anglican "Indian Training College" in Dauphin, Manitoba in 1958. (group photo from 1954 available at http://archives.algomau.ca/main/?q=node/17306).

32 From archival source Province of Saskatchewan archives R_874.1_1.6a, these are letters concerning Ahenakew Papers.

33 Buck, *Voices*, 95.

34 In the handwritten version Ahenakew spells the Cree for "the give-away dance" as mah-tah-e-to-win; in Standard Roman Orthography it is spelled as mâhtâhitowin.

35 Buck, *Voices*, 69.

36 Ahenakew, *Old Keyam*, 5.

37 Ahenakew, 35.

38 Cree spellings and definitions for this story from the *Online Cree Dictionary* at https://www.creedictionary.com/

39 When, for example, Ahenakew hears the guest cry out oskâyi—or "it is new," he has no idea why since the possessions the guests cry out to receive are clearly used, much as they might be if purchased from a garage sale. When the next morning he awakens to see Mahkesîs (the Fox), still awake, Ahenakew is intrigued but unable to understand why.

40 From unpublished archival sources.

41 Buck, *Voices*, 69.

42 Brundige, "Tanisi," 91.

43 Ahenakew, *Old Keyam*, 103.

44 Ahenakew, 103; in Buck's version (*Voices*) she writes that "he spoke well," 87.

45 Ahenakew, 103.

46 Brundige, "Tanisi," 85.

47 Cuthand, "Native Peoples," 383.

48   For other discussions of the role of respect in Cree Culture, see Laboucane-Benson et al., *Trauma*, 85–86; Wenger-Nabigon, "Cree Medicine Wheel," 153–54.
49   Brundige, "Tanisi," 41.
50   In a similar example, Winona Wheeler writes, in her Master's thesis that nineteenth-century Native catechists like Cree minister Charles Pratt (Akenootow) "syncretized Indigenous and European spirituality, skills, and ways of life in the best interests of his peoples' survival" ("Church Missionary," iii).
51   Brundige, "Tanisi," 85.
52   I'd like to thank Paul DePasquale for pointing out to me that the early history of contact between the Swampy Cree and Europeans, including treaty-making, confirms this point. As an example he has directed me to Louis Bird's discussion of the 1930 adhesion of Treaty Nine as recounted in *Telling Our Stories: Omushkego Legends and Histories from Hudson Bay* (2005).
53   Beeds, "Remembering," 62–63.
54   I suggest that the end date is 1915 because there is a reference to the thirtieth anniversary of the 1885 Frog Lake massacre.
55   Possibly "rot."
56   From archival sources, the second to last entry on Ahenakew's earliest notebook, on page 76 and 77, found in the "papers of Edward Ahenakew" in the Province of Saskatchewan Archives. Transcribed by Natalie Knight as part of The People and the Text.

Notes to Chapter Four

1   From "Edward Ahenakew" available at https://library.usask.ca/indigenous/history_essays/edward-ahenakew.php, in 1912 he also earned a Licentiate of Theology; see also Stan Cuthand, *Voices of the Plains Cree*, xi.
2   Cuthand, *Tapwe*.
3   Ahenakew's *Black Hawk*, despite being unpublished, is at the present time the first novel written by an Indigenous author in Canada; should anyone bring to light a novel written earlier than the 1914–1918 time period when this novel was composed, would then claim this title.
4   Iñupiaq Philosophy undergrad Rachel Taylor worked with Yurok and Diné PhD student Natalie Knight, to transcribe large portions of Ahenakew's work … after transcriptions they would read Ahenakew's words aloud to each other, to proofread their work and note words that were difficult to decipher, or note marginalia in the text. First, let's recognize that these Indigenous students did not study alongside rooms filled with other Indigenous students, did not have loads of Indigenous professors, did not read tons of Indigenous content in their curriculum—not because they wouldn't want to but because those Indigenous peers, profs, and publications were not there. For them to be able to read the poetry, the essays, the stories of a Cree intellectual— much of the work written a hundred years ago—from the hand of an Indigenous man who aspired to be a published writer, yet was seldom given the opportunity, affected both of them. Taylor has since completed a Masters of Publishing at SFU, is a busy freelance editor, and has helped establish the Indigenous Editors Association. Knight devoted a chapter of her dissertation to Ahenakew's discussion of economic ideas and completed her PhD in 2018, winning the Simon Fraser University Dean of Graduate Studies Convocation Medal.
5   McLeod, "Introduction," 8.
6   McLeod, 8.

7 In correspondence between David Miller and Donald Smith, Smith confirms that Dr. Pierce is Ryerson's Dr. Lorne Pierce (in the possession of the author).

8 Stan Cuthand references Ahenakew's letter to Paul Wallace, March 23, 1923 on page xix of his 1995 Preface.

9 Ahenakew, "Cree Trickster Tales," 309–53.

10 Edward Ahenakew, *Old Keyam*.

11 While unpublished manuscripts are typically put into quotation marks, in the interest of clarity, this manuscript italicizes all future references of the unpublished novel as *Black Hawk*, found in the Bibliography as Edward Ahenakew, "Black Hawk," Edward Ahenakew Papers, R-1, Folder 7, Part 2. Romance, Saskatchewan Archives Board, Regina.

12 In Ahenakew family history, some speculated that an uncle of Ahenakew's struggled with love gone wrong.

13 Caution to the reader since there are several duplications of names, not only in the unpublished novel *Black Hawk* but also in the unpublished manuscript *Old Keyam*, that features a main character named Old Keyam *and*, on top of this an edited, shortened, and abridged version referred to as "Old Keyam,"; "Old Keyam" is the version of the unpublished manuscript, *Old Keyam*, that was edited by Ruth M. Buck and published in 1973 as the second half of *Voices of the Plains Cree*. Buck created a different ending for "Old Keyam" than the one written by Ahenakew.

14 Ahenakew, *Black Hawk*, 4.

15 Ahenakew, 5.

16 Ahenakew, 5. Ruth M. Buck describes Edward Ahenakew's great-uncle Napaskis's travels with Donald Matheson and the Earl of Southesk around 1859 in Buck's *The Doctor Rode Side-Saddle*.

17 Ahenakew, *Black Hawk*, 6.

18 Ahenakew, 8. In Cree the word nâpêsis means "boy".

19 Ahenakew, "Genealogical Sketch of my Family," 14.

20 Ahenakew, 15.

21 Ahenakew, 18. In the notes in the 1973 edition of *Voices of the Plains Cree*, editor Ruth M. Buck points out that in about 1859 in Fort Carleton, the Earl of Southesk makes reference to a very bold intelligent young man named Napêsskes; likewise, the Cree cleric Reverend James Settee writes, in his unpublished journal dated at Fort Pelly in July 1861, the story of the death in battle of Napaskis: "A young half-Cree, half-Saulteau came ... he is mourning the death of his uncle Na-pâs-kis who had been killed just lately in the battle by the Blackfoot with twelve of his men. This Na-pâs-kis was a noted Warrior ... the bravest of the little plain Fort Chiefs" (as cited in Buck, *Voices*, 162).

22 See page 2 in "Genealogical Sketch of my Family" Ahenakew describes his mother's prayers for him as a young child, praying "to God asking Him to spare my life"; a similar episode is on page 15 in *Black Hawk*, regarding young Allan Hawk.

23 Ahenakew, *Black Hawk*, 67.

24 Ahenakew, 62.

25 The 1918 *Saskatoon Daily Star* article is also among the Ruth Buck papers in the Province of Saskatchewan archives, located in file R_20_II_3, p. 77.

26 It is not clear exactly when Ahenakew had to leave his medical studies due to ill-health but in an announcement in the *Saskatoon Daily Star*, there is an article on 31 May 1919 on "The Church and its Work" on page six; it states that "The announcement that Rev. Edward Ahenakew, of the Onion Lake Mission, had successfully passed the first Year examination in his medical course at Toronto has been received with pleasure

by his associates in the Diocese of Saskatchewan. Mr. Ahenakew is preparing himself for work as a medical missionary among the people of his own race in Saskatchewan."

27 While much of Ahenakew's *Black Hawk* exists in first or second draft, there are some inconsistencies worth noting. Ahenakew had not yet confirmed the names of some of his characters, most notably Helen/Ethel, Allan Hawk's love interest. The name Helen occurs 117 times in the narrative, once as the name of Allan Hawk's mother; however, five times at the end of the novel Ahenakew refers to the love interest as Ethel. The name "Alice," for the character who is sister to Helen and the love interest of Harry, occurs 45 times (plus four as the name of a different, younger character in an early section of the novel); periodically through the text the same character of Alice is referred to as Grace, a name Ahenakew uses 34 times.

28 Ahenakew, *Black Hawk*, 103.

29 Ahenakew, 104.

30 Buck, *Voices*, 1.

31 From archival source Province of Saskatchewan archive file R_874.1_I.6a, p. 28 (emphasis in the original). On January 28, 1969, in a letter to Dr. Spence, the Head of the Cultural Division of the Department of Indian Affairs and Northern Development, Buck comments: "These fourteen chapters have in fact been rewritten from the original twenty-five given in the outline with the first manuscript. Most of the original material is in the rough form, the first draft only, with corrections and cancellations. Some chapters are missing. I have been most scrupulous in my rewriting to use only the material from Edward Ahenakew's own manuscript including some short articles that are listed in the index as Item III" (28, underlining in original).

32 This quote comes from the entry on June, July, August 1963 of the "Papers of Edward Ahenakew", a chronology of the work Buck did over the years on this archive, beginning in May 1962 until October 1972, labelled R-1#1. In "A Checklist of the Papers of Edward Ahenakew" in the Saskatchewan Archives Board, Regina, 1993, it states that "The Edward Ahenakew Papers were donated to the Saskatchewan Archives Board by Ruth Matheson Buck at some time between April 1972 and March 1974. No Accession Number was assigned. The Collection Number is R-1. Material related to the collection may be found among the Ruth Matheson Buck Papers in Sections I and II of Collection R-20 and in Section 1 of Collection R-874.1 Both these collections are listed in GR 156. File #1 of the Collection contains a "Detailed Index" of the Ahenakew Papers prepared by Mrs. Buck and a chronology of her involvement with them" (ii–iii).

33 Kristina Bidwell also references Ruth M. Buck's decision to leave out passages by Ahenakew that she thought were too romantic. See Bidwell, "Cree Literature in Saskatchewan," 13. In fact, Buck leaves out more than just the references to romance in *Old Keyam*; Buck transforms the twenty-four chapters that Ahenakew sketches out into twelve. Of these twenty-four chapters, Buck notes that three have gone missing: Chapter V: Oo-pee-wa-me-wak or "Men who Dream"; Chapter XIII: The Saskatchewan League Convention; and Chapter XXI: Old Keyam on Married Life.

34 Ahenakew, *Old Keyam*, 151–52.

35 Ahenakew, 153. There is an error here because in this version the chapters are misnumbered and the chapter after "Management of Indian Moneys" and before "The Death of Old Keyam" called "Old Keyam on Married Life" is missing. In all Ahenakew had planned twenty-four chapters.

36 Buck, *Voices*, 107.

37 Buck, 107. In a comparison of the entire handwritten text by Ahenakew with the entire book that Buck edited, there is only one instance in the original manuscript

where the line "I wish" exists and it is halfway through the book, in a passage that says "I wish I had a grandfather like him" (page 73 of the original manuscript). Otherwise, there are three examples of "wishes" (pages 8, 10, 65), two examples of "wished" (9, 20), and one instance where Ahenakew used "wish" but scratched it out (90).

38   While there are multiple times when Keyam is referred to as Old Keyam, and two occasions when Keyam says that "I am old" (on pages 152 and 154 of the original handwritten manuscript *Old Keyam*), there is no point in the original text that includes the phrase "he is old" or "says that he is old."

39   Buck, *Voices*, 108.

40   In addition, there is a vignette in the final passage on the final page of Buck's *Voices of the Plains Cree*:

> His words surprise the Old Man, and Keyam dropped his head to hide his emotion. His hands fumbled at his belt, untying a leather pouch that glinted with new beads, the work of [his wife] Chohena's old fingers in an old art. "There's something here," he said, "Something that I have wanted to show you" (157).

In the entirety of the manuscript at no time are the following words used: "emotion"; "fumbled"; "leather pouch"; "beads"; or "old fingers". The only reference to "art" in the whole text is on page 135 of the original in reference to the "Indian art of heraldry."

41   "Old Keyam," that exists as the second half of *Voices of the Plains Cree*, 107–8, is written in quotation marks to indicate that this is the version edited by Ruth M. Buck.

42   Ahenakew, *Old Keyam*, 159, is italicized to indicate that this is the complete and unpublished version, existing among the Edward Ahenakew Papers at the Saskatchewan Archives Board.

43   Ahenakew spells Thunderbird as Peyasiw.

44   Ahenakew, *Old Keyam*, 159–60.

45   Ahenakew, 160.

46   Ahenakew, 163.

47   It is worth noting that Buck's decision to eliminate Ahenakew's words at the time of publication of *Voices of the Plains Cree* in 1973 occurs at the same time that Maria Campbell's publishers do not honour her wishes and instead remove a critically significant passage from *Halfbreed*. And it has taken roughly fifty years for a "search" for missing documents to be "found" and then made available to the publisher.

48   Ahenakew, 168.

49   Ahenakew, Scribbler 5, page 15, among the unpublished papers in the Edward Ahenakew Papers, Saskatchewan Archives Board.

Notes to Chapter Five

1   Farrell-Racette says he spoke "some Cree," in Farrell-Racette, "'Enclosing Some Snapshots,'" 271; Swain states that while Brady "eventually learned to understand Cree, he never learned to speak it," in Swain, "Victims," 4.

2   Brady worked with four others—Peter Tomkins, Felix Calliou, Malcolm Norris, and Joseph Dion—to secure Métis rights in the province of Alberta in the 1930s. Together they were referred to as the Famous Five.

3   Anne Acco, for example, talks about how her family had a dry warehouse in Cumberland House where Jim stored some of his books; the benefit to Anne was that she had a library at her fingertips. See Acco, "Interview."

4   Sherry Farrell-Racette, in her 2019 article "'Enclosing Some Snapshots': James Patrick Brady, Photography, and Political Activism," lists the size of the library as "over 2000"

(286); she quotes Andre Bouthillette in an interview with Murray Dobbin that took place on January 13, 1978 Bouthillette, "Interview," 269–87.

5   For a list of Brady's book collection, see his handwritten list, available at www .thepeopleandthetext.ca

6   Books for Study organized by the Toronto Writers Group included Frederick Philip Grove's *Our Daily Bread* (1928), *Fruits of the Earth* (1935), and *The Master of the Mill* (1944), as well as titles from Robert Stead (1925), Patrick Slater (1933), Irene Baird (1939), Hugh MacLennan (1941, 1945), Thomas Raddall (1942), Selwyn Dewdney (1946), and Dyson Carter (1950). See James Brady Fonds M-125-F55 at the Glenbow Museum and Archives.

7   Marcel Giraud was a professor of North American civilization at the Collège de France in Paris who studied the Métis in western Canada in the 1930s.

8   For the letter from Bruce Peel to James Brady, see James Brady Fonds M-125-F39.

9   See "About Bruce Peel," http://peel.library.ualberta.ca/brucepeel.html.

10 For a discussion of Brady's interactions with Marcel Giraud and Giraud's influential yet flawed book, see Farrell-Racette, "Enclosing Some Snapshots."

11 Historical notes by James Brady, M-125-39, Series 5: First Nations and Metis files, James Brady fonds, Glenbow Library and Archives, University of Calgary, accessed August 6, 2019, https://glenbow.ucalgary.ca/finding-aid/james-brady-fonds/

   Historical notes. 1932–1959. File consists of notes, histories and drafts by Brady, minutes. Lists, transcripts and correspondence regarding Metis and First Nations in Alberta and Saskatchewan, Metis history, Metis Association of Alberta, St Paul Half- Breed Reserve, Louis Riel, Northwest Rebellion, co-operatives, land tenure and property rights.

12 Brady confirms his plans to write a "short history of the activities of the Alberta Metis Association during the years I was associated with them" in the fifth interview with Art Davis in 1960 (see page 5 of this interview at http://hdl.handle.net/10294/556)

13 See James Brady Fonds, Glenbow Museum and Archives.

14 For example, on December 19, 1944 he records: "At Brakkenstein [Netherlands]. Spent the afternoon with the monks at the monastery of St. Ciroure. They claim the local population is 90% pro-Nazi. Went back to billets in the evening and read Ludwig Renn." War diary by James Brady, M-125-1, Series 1: Diaries, James Brady fonds, Glenbow Library and Archives, University of Calgary. https://glenbow.ucalgary.ca/finding-aid/james-brady-fonds/.

15 Miscellaneous notes by James Brady, M-125-48, Series 5: Historical notes, James Brady fonds, Glenbow Library and Archives, University of Calgary. https://glenbow .ucalgary.ca/finding-aid/james-brady-fonds/

16 Gratitude to Margery Fee for this point; to get a sense of the publication history of the study of William Blake in Canada see the Editor's Preface in *The Collected Works of Northrop Frye*, edited by Nicholas Halmi.

17 Ken Hatt to Kathy Quandt, August 7, 1975, 4. Papers in possession of the author.

18 James Brady, "The Wisdom of Papasschayo: A Cree Medicine Man," transcribed by David Morin, *The Virtual Museum of Métis History and Culture*, Gabriel Dumont Institute of Native Studies and Applied Research, http://www.metismuseum.ca/resource .php/03831

19 Dwayne Donald, "We Need a New Story: Walking and the wâhkôhtowin Imagination," *Journal of the Canadian Association for Curriculum Studies* 18, no. 2, (2021): 58–59.

20 In 2022, it is hard not to hear the warning in Papasschayo's words.

21 In the 6 May 1963 letter from Charles S. Brant, the letterhead signals that he writes from the Department of Sociology and then a typist has added "And Anthropology",

signalling the recent addition of this discipline to the University of Alberta; Brant signed his letters to Brady as "Charley".

22 The only version of this text available among Brady's papers is an eleven-page story called "The Wisdom of Papasschayo: a Cree Medicine Man."

23 See James Brady fonds for correspondence with Charles Brant:

> The fact that I myself would seek a naturalistic, empirical explanation of such phenomena, rather than accept easily a supernaturalistic explanation of such as clairvoyance, does not make the document any the less important. My hunch would be that, although Papasschayo was an illiterate Indian without knowledge of any European language, the circumstances of life and of those times were such that, in all probability, he had heard others talking about the tide of events in Europe preceding the first World War.
>
> You are right in assuming that my scientific training and attendant skepticism makes me tend to reject occult explanations of anything. But as historical materialists I think this view in incumbent upon us. Can we, for instance, reject the "pie in the sky" Christian view of life and after-life as nonsense and political dope-peddling—but at the same time, accept occultistic, supernaturalistic explanations of events by medicine-men, just because the latter are Indians, Africans, Australian aboriginals, or whatever? I think we have to be consistent."

24 Hugh Dempsey, "1963 Letter from Hugh Dempsey to James Brady," *The Virtual Museum of Métis History and Culture*, Gabriel Dumont Institute of Native Studies and Applied Research, http://www.metismuseum.ca/resource.php/03863

25 For a history of Papaschase First Nation, see Papaschase First Nation, "Homepage," accessed August 6, 2020, https://papaschase.ca.

26 Thanks to Mischa Reder-Davis, who counted the list of books made by Brady and found 4,406 titles listed.

27 Intriguingly there are five separate interviews of Brady by Art Davis in 1960 available online. The interviews were transcribed by Heather Yaworski and are posted on the University of Regina oURspace webpage. Ostensibly a general account of Brady's life and his memories of Métis history, I have not found documentation that these interviews have a direct connection to the contracted life-history.

28 Dobbin, *The One-and-a-Half Men*.

29 Murray Dobbin records that "the disappearance and death of Jim Brady and Abbie Halkett remain a mystery. Speculation about the disappearance produced many hypotheses, some pure fantasy such as the claims that the men travelled surreptitiously to Cuba, were plucked from the earth by a flying saucer, or that they were murdered by the CIA" (Dobbin, *The One-and-a-Half Men*, 249).

30 Frank Tomkins, in conversation with the author, 2002.

31 Murray Dobbin, in the process of writing about Norris and Brady, kept notes of his research, including interviews he made about the disappearance (and likely death) of Brady and Halkett. Murray Dobbin, "Brady's Demise."

32 For a discussion of the landscape of Northern Saskatchewan, see the autobiography of Warren Cariou, *Lake of the Prairies: A Story of Belonging* (Toronto: Doubleday Canada, 2002).

33 For a recount of the full search see Nest with Reder and Bell, *Cold Case North*.

34 Thornton, "The National Policy," 160.

35 Bouthillette, "Interview," 8.

36 1978 interview with Liora Salter by Murray Dobbin: http://drc.usask.ca/projects/legal_aid/file/resource321-2c7a0414.pdf also http://www.metismuseum.ca/resource.php/01132

Notes to Chapter Six

1   See Wawryshyn, "Eyes of Province."
2   Drew Hayden Taylor outlines the history of this artistic explosion in Hayden Taylor, "Alive and Well," 29–37.
3   See also Warley for a discussion of notable books on residential schools published since the 1970s. Warley, "Before *Secret Path*," 285–299.
4   There are obviously similarities between the emergence of Canadian literature and Native literatures as fields of study: a lack of respect, never mind prestige, that the critic must fight against; the need to have new works not only taught in the classroom but taught proficiently; the fight against hegemonic forces that have dismissed these literatures. But I want to make the case that this current situation is less similar than it appears. If Expo '67 in Montreal, coinciding with Canada's Centennial, was a critical moment when this country began to think of itself as a nation, then the promotion of Canadian literature would reaffirm this identity. But in 2000 there was no bastion of Indigenous scholars able to lobby for the teaching of Indigenous literatures in universities. This is a constituency that we in the field are working on even now. This is not to diminish the efforts of those who worked to include Native literature in classrooms. In fact, the situation is very complex for the non-Indigenous teacher in this field. While I leave further discussion of this for another project, I quote Jo-Ann Episkenew when she writes:

> Indeed, any class on Shakespeare would not be complete without a comprehensive examination of the political and religious situation in Elizabethan England, no doubt comprised of information that the instructor has gathered from books in the library. These scholars need not worry that there just might be an Elizabethan enrolled in his or her class and that Elizabethan student just might dispute the information given in the lecture. However, this might very well occur in a class on contemporary Aboriginal literature. (Episkenew, "Socially Responsible Criticism," 65).

5   While I always wanted to complete doctoral work, when I began my PhD in 2001 at the University of British Columbia, my family moved into family housing from Stó:lō territory in the Fraser Valley where we had spent almost a decade; my oldest son was beginning his Bachelor of Science degree, my middle son was in elementary school, my youngest son was in kindergarten, and my husband had a long commute across the city and then on the highway. I acknowledge the personal sacrifices each of them made to support my work.
6   This is not true in the Library of Congress, where it is impossible to search for Musqueam or Tsleil-Waututh sources separately, having to look instead for the category of "Coast Salish"; For a discussion of the history and critique of the term "Coast Salish" see Alexandra Harmon's essay "Coast Salish History," 30–54.
7   An example of this is "The Women's Warrior Song" that is very well known and often sung at events across the continent; it was gifted to the public, in honour of Indigenous women, by Martina Pierre, from Lil'wat First Nation.
8   It is for this reason that a lot of inter-tribal gatherings in the lower mainland of British Columbia rely on the more open ceremonies of the Sweatlodge rather than offend the privacy and protocols of local peoples.
9   Warrior, *Tribal Secrets*, xiv.
10 I am grateful to fellow graduate student and friend, Alannah Young, who worked at the time at the First Nations House of Learning and passed on to me a transcript of the speech. Another copy was deposited in the Xwi7xwa Library at UBC.

11 Cardinal's title, "Einew kis-keetum-awin" is spelled in SRO as "iyiniw kiskêyihtamowin."

12 Cardinal, "Einew Kis-Kee-Tum-Awin."

13 The question: "awina maga kiya?" in SRO is "awîna mâka kiya."

14 Cardinal's discussion of a similar question, "*Awina maga kee anow* [awîna mâka kiyânaw]?" or "Who is it that we really are?" is recorded in his essay "Nation-Building: Reflections of a Nihiyow," in Paul W. DePasquale, ed., *Natives and Settlers Now and Then: Historical Issues and Current Perspectives on Treaties and Land Claims in Canada* (Edmonton, AB: University of Alberta Press, 2007). My thanks to Paul DePasquale, editor of this collection of essays in which this article resides, for pointing this out to me. For further discussion on the definitions of nêhiyaw, see also Cardinal's essay, "A Canadian What the Hell It's All About." *An Anthology of Canadian Native Literature in English*, 2nd ed., ed. Daniel David Moses and Terry Goldie (Toronto: Oxford University Press, 1998), 211–17.

15 Cardinal's phrase neehiyow neyah is spelled in SRO as nêhiyaw niya.

16 Cardinal, "Einew Kis-Kee-Tum-Awin." [iyiniw kiskêyihtamowin]

17 Gooderham, *I am an Indian*.

18 Waubageshig, *The Only Good Indian*.

19 Cardinal's phrases, ta ni ki maga nee hi youw kee tig a wee yin? tansi ee twee maga? are spelled in SRO as tânêhki mâka nêhiyaw kâ- itikawiyan? tânisi ê-itwêhk mâka?

20 Cardinal, "Einew Kis-Kee-Tum-Awin." [iyiniw kiskêyihtamowin]

21 The relationship to knowledge that the Elder outlines depends on different assumptions than that which direct Western academic inquiry. Cardinal's Elder understands research to be much less based on competition and isolation and he is not promoting the rhetoric of "academic excellence," "merit," "specialization," and "academic freedom"—none of which are transparent terms but rather ones loaded with cultural assumptions that anyone has access to any "knowledge," as long as it neither infringes on someone else's copyright or plagiarizes from someone else's work. Even initiatives that the institution develops to encourage cooperation and interdisciplinarity are undermined by the structure of the place itself. For example, some classes and departments might structure assignments to accommodate cooperative learning; even so, it is the individual student's grade that determines his or her ability to get into higher degree programs or secure funding. Even though universities may outwardly espouse interdisciplinary inquiry, the disciplines largely remain as the institutional foundation.

22 Much thanks to Arden Ogg who alerted me to the controversy about the Four Worlds definition and the work by Kevin Brosseau.

23 Brousseau, "Cree Folk Etymologies."

24 Go to https://creeliteracy.org/2012/01/20/another-story-from-solomon-ratt/ to hear a recording of Ratt telling the story. Ratt, "I'm Not an Indian."

25 Cardinal, "Einew Kis-Kee-Tum-Awin." [iyiniw kiskêyihtamowin], 7.

26 Brass, *Two Worlds*.

27 Cuthand, "On Nelson's Text," 194–95.

28 Armstrong and Grauer, *Native Poetry*, xv. They later heard it was Gordon Williams.

29 Armstrong and Grauer, xv.

30 Armstrong and Grauer, xvi.

31 Armstrong and Grauer, xvi.

32 Armstrong and Grauer, xvii.

33 Armstrong and Grauer, xix.

34 Armstrong and Grauer, xx.

35 Continuing this discussion, in what became known as the "Appropriation of Voice
    Debates," was the subsequent article by Lenore Keeshig-Tobias in the *Globe and
    Mail* entitled "Stop Stealing Native Stories" (A7) ; St. Peter, "'Women's Truth'" and
    "Feminist Afterwords."
36 Cameron, *Daughters of Copper Woman*.
37 Maracle, "Native Myths," 182–87.
38 Maracle attributes these quotes to Jeannette Armstrong, Chrystos, and editor Viola
    Thomas, respectively. Maracle, 185.
39 While Kinsella is most famous for the novel *Shoeless Joe* (Boston: Houghton Mifflin
    Company, 1982), which is the basis of the motion picture *Field of Dreams*, he is also
    the author of several collections of short stories situated on a fictionalized Hobbema
    Indian Reservation.
40 Quaife's first novel, *Bone Bird* (1989), won the Commonwealth Writers Prize for
    Best First Book. The novel is about a young woman whose "Indian" grandmother is
    a medicine woman who shares traditional teachings with her.
41 For a comprehensive discussion of this moment, including the contributions of
    Lenore Keeshig-Tobias, see Fee, "The Trickster Moment", 59–76; see also Emberley,
    Thresholds of Difference.
42 Programme des activités, 3rd International Feminist Book Fair, June 14 to 19, 1988, Mon-
    treal, 11, https://issuu.com/rimaathar/docs/programme_des_activites_3rdinternat
43 This would be Luci Tapahonso reading "Hills Brothers Coffee." Programme, 11.
44 Eakin, *Fictions in Autobiography*, 97.
45 McLeod, "Exploring Cree Narrative Memory," 74, 77–78.
46 See Maracle's "You Become the Trickster," from *Sojourner's Truth and Other Stories*,
    1990, 11–13.

Bibliography

"About Bruce Peel," Peel's Prairie Provinces, University of Alberta, http://peel .library.ualberta.ca/brucepeel.html, accessed 6 August 2019.

Absolon, Kathleen E. *Kaandossiwin: How We Come to Know.* Halifax, NS: Fernwood, 2011.

Acco, Anne. *Interview with Hartmut Lutz.* By Hartmut Lutz. The People and the Text, October 13, 1990. http://thepeopleandthetext.ca/islandora/object/ tpatt%3A2fc13df1-6c5d-4a20-a420-bd94b5bd5e8a

Adams, Howard. *Prison of Grass: Canada from the Native Point of View.* Toronto, ON: New Press, 1975.

Ahenakew, Alice. *âh-âyîtaw isi ê-kî-kiskêyihtahkik maskihkiy = They Knew Both Sides of Medicine: Cree Tales of Curing and Cursing Told by Alice Ahenakew.* Edited and translated by Freda Ahenakew and H. C. Wolfart. Winnipeg, MB: University of Manitoba Press, 2000.

Ahenakew, Edward. "Black Hawk." Edward Ahenakew Papers, R-1, Folder 7, Part 2. Romance. Saskatchewan Archives Board, Regina.

——. "Cree Trickster Tales." *Journal of American Folklore* 42, no. 166 (1929): 309–53.

——. Edward Ahenakew Papers. Saskatchewan Archives Board, Regina.

——. Genealogical Sketch of My Family. Boas Collection 64, Phillips Fund, 1948. Franz Boas Linguistics Collection, American Philosophical Society Library (APS), Philadelphia.

——. Old Keyam. Edward Ahenakew Papers, file R_1_Ahenakew_11_Old Keyam_Manuscript. Saskatchewan Archives Board, Regina.

——. "The Story of Rev. Canon Edward Ahenakew" Edward Ahenakew Papers, collection call number R2-5. Saskatchewan Archives Board, Regina.

——. "The Story of the Ahenakews." *Saskatchewan History* 18 (1964): 12–23.

——. *Voices of the Plains Cree.* Edited by Ruth M. Buck. Rev. ed. Regina, SK: Canadian Plains Research Center, 1995.

Ahenakew, Freda, and H. Christoph Wolfart, eds. *Our Grandmothers' Lives: As Told in Their Own Words.* Saskatoon, SK: Fifth House Publishers, 1992.

Angel, Michael. *Preserving the Sacred: Historical Perspectives on the Ojibwa Midewiwin.* Winnipeg, MB: University of Manitoba Press, 2002.

Apess, William. *A Son of the Forest: The Experience of William Apess, A Native of the Forest, Comprising a Notice of the Pequod Tribe of Indians, Written by Himself.* New York, NY: Self-published, 1829.

Archibald, Jo-ann. "Coyote Learns to Make a Storybasket: The Place of First Nations Stories in Education." PhD diss., Simon Fraser University, 1997. http://summit.sfu.ca/item/7275

Archibald-Barber, Jesse Rae. *kisiskâciwan: Indigenous Voices from Where the River Flows Swiftly*. Regina, SK: University of Regina Press, 2018.

Armstrong, Jeannette C., and Lally Grauer, eds. *Native Poetry in Canada: A Contemporary Anthology*. Peterborough, ON: Broadview, 2001.

Barman, Jean. *On the Cusp of Contact: Gender, Space and Race in the Colonization of British Columbia*. Madeira Park, BC: Harbour Publishing, 2020.

Bataille, Gretchen M., and Kathleen Mullen Sands. *American Indian Women: Telling Their Lives*. Lincoln, NE: University of Nebraska Press, 1984.

Beeds, Tasha. "Remembering the Poetics of Ancient Sound kistêsinâw/wîsahkêcâhk's maskihkiy (Elder Brother's Medicine)." In *Indigenous Poetics in Canada*, edited by Neal McLeod, 61–71. Waterloo, ON: Wilfrid Laurier University Press, 2014.

———. "Rethinking Edward Ahenakew's Intellectual Legacy: Expressions of nêhiyawimâmitonêyihcikan (Cree Consciousness)." In *Mixed Blessings: Indigenous Encounters with Christianity in Canada*, edited by Tolly Bradford and Chelsea Horton, 119–141. Vancouver, BC: University of British Columbia Press, 2016.

Bell, Gloria Jane. "Gramophone, Masinatahikan—Typewriter, Press, Our Mother(s) Tongue: Reflections on Indigenous (First Nations and Métis) Literacies and Media." *KULA: Knowledge Creation, Dissemination, and Preservation Studies* 5, no. 1 (2021). https://doi.org/10.18357/kula.142

Bell, Robert. Robert Bell Fonds, National Archives of Canada, MG 29 B15 Vol. 54 and relevant files.

Bidwell, Kristina Fagan. "'Our New Storytellers': Cree Literature in Saskatchewan." In *The Literary History of Saskatchewan: Volume 1 Beginnings* edited by David Carpenter. Regina, SK: Coteau Books, 2013.

Bird, John R. E. "'Stranger in a Strange Land': Cultural Hybridity and Mimicry in George Copway's Engagement with Christianity, Freemasonry, and Literacy." PhD diss., University of Saskatchewan, 2017.

Bird, Louis. *Telling Our Stories: Omushkego Legends and Histories from Hudson Bay*. Edited by Jennifer S. H. Brown, Paul Warren DePasquale, and Mark F. Ruml with contributions by Roland Bohr, Anne Lindsay, and Donna G. Sutherland. Toronto, ON: University of Toronto Press, 2005.

Blaeser, Kimberly M. "Native Literature: Seeking a Critical Center" in *Looking At the Words of Our People: First Nations Analysis of Literature*, edited by Jeannette Armstrong. Penticton, BC: Theytus Books, 1993. 51–62.

Borrows, John Joseph, and Leonard Ian Rotman. *Aboriginal Legal Issues: Cases, Materials & Commentary*. 2nd ed. Toronto, ON: LexisNexis Butterworths, 2003.

Borrows, Lindsay Keegitah. "On the Road Home: Stories and Reflections from Neyaashiinigiming". In *Centering Anishinaabeg Studies: Understanding the World through Stories*, edited by Jill Doerfler, Heidi Kiiwetinepinesiik Stark, and Niigaanwewidam James Sinclair, 397–407. Winnipeg, MB: University of Manitoba Press, 2013.

Bouthillette, Andre. *Andre Bouthillette interview*. By Murray Dobbin. Saskatoon, Saskatchewan, January 13, 1978. 22, IH-424/424A, SAB. Quoted in Sherry

Farrell-Racette, "'Enclosing Some Snapshots': James Patrick Brady, Photography, and Political Activism," *History of Photography* 42, no. 3: 269–287.

Brady, James. James Brady Fonds, Glenbow Museum and Archives.

———. "Papers. The People and the Text Collection." Canadian Writing and Research Collaboratory. Accessed August 6, 2019. http://thepeopleandthe text.ca/islandora/object/tpatt%3Ajimbrady

Brady, James [J.P.]. "The Wisdom of Papasschayo, A Cree Medicine Man." The Virtual Museum of Métis History and Culture. Gabriel Dumont Institute of Native Studies and Applied Research, copyright October 18, 2004. http://www.metismuseum.ca/resource.php/03831

Brass, Eleanor. *I Walk in Two Worlds*. Calgary, AB: Glenbow Museum, 1987.

Brotherston, Gordon. *The Image of the New World: The American Continent Portrayed in Native Texts*. London: Thames & Hudson, 1979.

Brousseau, Kevin. "Cree Folk Etymologies." *Kepin's Cree Language Blog*. March 29, 2020. https://creelanguage.wordpress.com/2020/03/29/cree-folk-etymologies/

Brown, Jennifer S.H. "James Settee and his Cree Tradition: An Indian Camp at the Mouth of Nelson River Hudsons Bay." *Algonquian Papers-Archive* 8 (1977).

Brumble, H. David, III. *American Indian Autobiography*. Berkeley, CA: University of California Press, 1988.

———. *An Annotated Bibliography of American Indian and Eskimo Autobiographies*. Lincoln, NE: University of Nebraska Press, 1981.

Brundige, Lorraine. "Tanisi Isinisitohtamahk Kitaskino: Cree Philosophy Akwa Kayaskiacimowin." PhD diss., University of Oregon, 2004.

Buck, Ruth M. *The Doctor Rode Side-Saddle*. Regina: University of Regina Press, 2003.

———. "Introduction to the 1973 Edition" *Voices of the Plains Cree* by Edward Ahenakew, 1–8. Edited by Ruth M. Buck. Rev. ed. Regina, SK: Canadian Plains Research Center, 1995.

———, ed. "The Story of the Ahenakews." *Saskatchewan History* 17, no. 1 (1964): 12–23.

Cameron, Anne. *Daughters of Copper Woman*. Vancouver, BC: Press Gang Publishers, 1985.

Campbell, Maria. *Halfbreed*. Toronto, ON: McClelland & Stewart, 1973. Reprinted 2019.

———. "Kiasyno Akuâ Nehiawatsowin: Old Man and Cree Life Ways." As cited in Stevenson (Wheeler), Winona L. "Decolonizing Tribal Histories." PhD diss., University of California, Berkeley, 2000. Unpublished manuscript in the possession of Winona Wheeler. Last modified 1999. Microsoft Word file.

———. "Ni'wahkomakanak: All My Relations." Speech, Federation of Social Science and Humanities Big Thinking at Virtual Congress 2021, Online, 2 June 2021.

———. *Stories of the Road Allowance People*. Penticton, BC: Theytus, 1995.

Cardinal, Harold. "Einew Kis-Kee-Tum-Awin: Indigenous People's Knowledge." Speech, Assembly of First Nations Special Chiefs Assembly. Renaissance Vancouver Hotel Harbourside, Vancouver, BC, March 29, 2005.

———. "Nation-Building: Reflections of a Nihiyow [Cree]." In *Natives and Settlers Now and Then: Historical Issues and Current Perspectives on Treaties and Land Claims in Canada*, edited by Paul W. DePasquale, 65–77. Edmonton, AB: University of Alberta Press, 2007.

———. *The Unjust Society: The Tragedy of Canada's Indians*. Edmonton, AB: M. G. Hurtig, 1969.

Cariou, Warren. *Lake of the Prairies: A Story of Belonging*. Toronto, ON: Doubleday Canada, 2002.

———. "On Critical Humility." *Studies in American Indian Literatures*, 32, nos. 3–4 (Fall-Winter 2020): 1–12.

Carter, Sarah. *Aboriginal People and Colonizers of Western Canada to 1900*. Toronto, ON: University of Toronto Press, 1999.

Chacón, Gloria Elizabeth. *Indigenous Cosmolectics: Kab'awil and the Making of Maya and Zapotec Literatures*. Chapel Hill, NC: University of North Carolina Press, 2018.

Chrystos. *Not Vanishing*. Vancouver, BC: Press Gang Publishers, 1988.

"The Church and its Work." *Saskatoon Daily Star*, 31 May 1919, 6.

Copway, George. "The Life, History and Travels of Kah-ge-ga-gah-bowh (1847)." In *Masterpieces of American Indian Literature*, edited by Willis G. Regnier, 1–142. Lincoln, NE: University of Nebraska Press, 2005.

Coulthard, Glen Sean. *Red Skin, White Masks: Rejecting the Colonial Politics of Recognition*. Minneapolis, MN: University of Minnesota Press, 2014.

Crasnow, Sharon. "Contemporary Standpoint Theory: Tensions, Integrations, and Extensions". In *The Bloomsbury Companion to Analytic Feminism*, edited by Pieranna Garavaso, 188–211. New York, NY: Bloomsbury Publishing, 2018.

Cuthand, Doug. *Tapwe: Selected Columns of Doug Cuthand*. Penticton, BC: Theytus Books, 2005.

Cuthand, Stan. "The Native Peoples of the Prairie Provinces in the 1920s and 1930s." In *Sweet Promises: A Reader on Indian-White Relations in Canada*, edited by J. R. Miller, 381–92. Toronto, ON: University of Toronto Press, 1991.

———. "On Nelson's Text." In *"The Orders of the Dreamed": George Nelson on Cree and Northern Ojibwa Religion and Myth, 1823*, edited by Jennifer S. H. Brown and Robert Brightman, 189–98. Winnipeg, MB: University of Manitoba Press, 2004.

———. Preface to *Voices of the Plains Cree* by Edward Ahenakew, edited by Ruth M. Buck, rev. ed., vii–xx. Regina, SK: Canadian Plains Research Center, 1995.

Deloria, Philip J. *Playing Indian*. New Haven, CT: Yale University Press, 1998.

Dempsey, Hugh. "1963 Letter from Hugh Dempsey to James Brady." The Virtual Museum of Métis History and Culture. Gabriel Dumont Institute of Native Studies and Applied Research, copyright October 22, 2004. http://www.metismuseum.ca/resource.php/03863

DePasquale, Paul W., ed. *Natives and Settlers Now and Then: Historical Issues and Current Perspectives on Treaties and Land Claims in Canada*. Edmonton, AB: University of Alberta Press, 2007.

DiNova, Joanne. *Spiraling Webs of Relation: Movements Toward an Indigenist Criticism*. Abingdon, UK: Routledge, 2005.

Dion, Joseph F. *My Tribe, the Crees*. Edited by Hugh A. Dempsey. Calgary, AB: Glenbow Museum, 1979.

Dobbin, Murray. "Brady's Demise." *The Virtual Museum of Métis History and Culture*. Gabriel Dumont Institute of Native Studies and Applied Research, copyright October 22, 2004. www.metismuseum.ca/resource.php/03865

——. *The One-and-a-Half Men: The Story of Jim Brady and Malcolm Norris, Métis Patriots of the 20th Century*. Vancouver, BC: New Star, 1981.

Doerfler, Jill, Heidi Kiiwetinepinesiik Stark, and Niigaanwewidam James Sinclair, eds. *Centering Anishinaabeg Studies: Understanding the World through Stories*. Winnipeg, MB: University of Manitoba Press, 2013.

Donald, Dwayne. "We Need a New Story: Walking and the wâhkôhtowin Imagination." *Journal of the Canadian Association for Curriculum Studies (JCAS)* 18, no. 2, (2021): 53–63.

Doolittle, Robyn. "The Unfounded Effect," *Globe* (Toronto), 8 December 2017.

Dorion, Leah. "Peter Tomkins, Jr.: Métis Socialist, 1899-1970." *Eagle Feather News*, Dec. 1999–January 2000. Reprinted in Next Year Country (blog), May 25, 2010. http://nextyearcountrynews.blogspot.com/2010/05/peter-tomkins-jr-metis-socialist.html

Dumont, Marilyn. *A Really Good Brown Girl*. London, ON: Brick, 1996.

Eakin, Paul John. *Fictions in Autobiography: Studies in the Art of Self-Invention*. Princeton, NJ: Princeton University Press, 1985.

——. *How Our Lives Become Stories: Making Selves*. Ithaca, NY: Cornell University Press, 1999.

——. "Relational Selves, Relational Lives: Autobiography and the Myth of Autonomy." In *How Our Lives Become Stories: Making Selves*, 43–99. Ithaca, NY: Cornell University Press, 1999.

"Edward Ahenakew" Aboriginal Research Resources, University of Saskatchewan Library, https://library.usask.ca/indigenous/history_essays/edward-ahenakew.php

Edwards, Brendan Frederick R. *Paper Talk: A History of Libraries, Print Culture and Aboriginal Peoples in Canada Before 1960*. Lanham, MD: Scarecrow, 2005.

Emberley, Julia. *Thresholds of Difference: Feminist Critique, Native Women's Writings, Post-Colonial Theory*. Toronto, ON: University of Toronto Press, 1993.

Episkenew, Jo-Ann. "Socially Responsible Criticism: Aboriginal Literature, Ideology, and the Literary Canon." In *Creating Community: A Roundtable on Canadian Aboriginal Literature*, edited by Renate Eigenbrod and Jo-Ann Episkenew, 51–68. Penticton, BC: Theytus Books and Bearpaw, 2002.

Farrell-Racette, Sherry. "'Enclosing Some Snapshots': James Patrick Brady, Photography, and Political Activism," *History of Photography* 42, no. 3 (2018): 269–287.

Fee, Margery. "The Trickster Moment, Cultural Appropriation, and the Liberal Imagination in Canada." In *Troubling Tricksters: Revisioning Critical*

Conversations, edited by Deanna Reder and Linda M. Morra, 59–76. Waterloo, ON: Wilfrid Laurier University Press, 2010.

Francis, Daniel. *The Imaginary Indian: The Image of the Indian in Canadian Culture*. Vancouver: Arsenal Pulp, 1992.

"Frank Tomkins." *The Virtual Museum of Métis History and Culture*. Gabriel Dumont Institute of Native Studies and Applied Research, copyright December 14, 2004. http://www.metismuseum.ca/resource.php/03369

Frye, Northrup. *Fearful Symmetry: A Study of William Blake*, edited by Nicholas Halmi. Princeton, NJ: Princeton University Press, 1947.

George, Chief Earl Maquinna. *Living on the Edge: Nuu-Chah-Nulth History from an Ahousaht Chief's Perspective*. Winlaw, BC: Sono Nis, 2003.

Giraud, Marcel. *The Metis in the Canadian West*, translated by George Woodcock. Edmonton: University of Alberta Press, 1986.

Gooderham, Kent. *I am an Indian*. Toronto, ON: J. M. Dent, 1969.

Goulet, Linda M., and Keith N. Goulet. *Teaching Each Other: Nehinuw Concepts and Indigenous Pedagogies*. Vancouver, BC: University of British Columbia Press, 2014.

Graham, Maryemma and Mercedes Lucero. "Lifewriting." In *The Routledge Handbook to the Culture and Media of the Americas*, edited by Wilfried Raussert, Giselle Liza Anatol, Sebastian Thies, Sarah Corona Berkin, José Carlos Lozano, 121–135. London, UK: Routledge, 2020.

Gunew, Sneja. "Authenticity and the Writing Cure: Reading Some Migrant Women's Writing." *Poetics* 17, nos. 1–2 (April 1988): 81–97.

Halfe, Louise. *Crooked Good*. Regina, SK: Coteau, 2007.

———. "Keynote Address: The Rolling Head's 'Grave' yard." *Studies in Canadian Literature* 31 (2006): 65–74.

Hallowell, Gerald, ed. *The Oxford Companion to Canadian History*. Don Mills, ON: Oxford University Press, 2004.

Hambling, Skip. "Constitutional Update: London, England—AMNSIS Has Made It." *The New Breed* (May 1981): 8–10.

Haraway, Donna. *Simians, Cyborgs, and Women: the Reinvention of Nature*. New York, NY: Routledge, 1991.

Harding, Sandra, ed. *The Feminist Standpoint Theory Reader: Intellectual and Political Controversies*. New York, NY: Routledge, 2004.

Harmon, Alexandra. "Coast Salish History" in *Be of Good Mind: Essays on the Coast Salish*. UBC Press, 2007. 30–54.

Highway, Tomson. *Kiss of the Fur Queen*. Toronto, ON: Doubleday, 1998.

Huhndorf, Shari. *Going Native: Indians in the American Cultural Imagination*. Ithaca, NY: Cornell University Press, 2001.

Innes, Robert Alexander. *Elder Brother and the Law of the People*. Winnipeg. MB: University of Manitoba Press, 2013.

"Interview with Liora Salter by Murray Dobbin" 1978: http://drc.usask.ca/projects/legal_aid/file/resource321-2c7a0414.pdf also http://www.metismuseum.ca/resource.php/01132

"James Brady 5" Interview with Art Davis, *Our Space*, University of Regina. 1960. http://hdl.handle.net/10294/556

Jewitt, John R. *White Slaves of Maquinna: John R. Jewitt's Narrative of Capture and Confinement at Nootka*. Middletown: Seth Richards, 1815. Reprinted. Surrey, BC: Heritage House, 1987.

Joe, Rita. *Song of Rita Joe: Autobiography of a Mi'kmaq Poet*. Charlottetown, PE: Ragweed, 1996.

Johnson, E. Pauline (Tekahionwake). "The Song My Paddle Sings." In *Flint and Feather*, 31–32. Toronto: Musson, 1912.

Jones, Peter. *Life and Travels of Kah-ke-wa-quo-na-by (Rev. Peter Jones), Wesleyan Missionary*. Toronto, ON: A. Green, 1860.

Joseph, Bob. *21 Things You Didn't Know About the Indian Act: Helping Canadians Make Reconciliation with Indigenous Peoples a Reality*. Port Coquitlam, BC: Indigenous Relations Press, 2018.

Justice, Daniel Heath. *Why Indigenous Literatures Matter*. Waterloo, ON: Wilfrid Laurier University Press, 2018.

Keeshig-Tobias, Lenore. "Stop Stealing Native Stories." *The Globe and Mail*, January 26, 1990. Reprinted in *Introduction to Indigenous Literary Criticism in Canada* edited by Heather Macfarlane and Armand Garnet Ruffo. Peterborough, ON: Broadview Press, 2016.

King, Thomas. *The Truth About Stories: A Native Narrative*. Toronto, ON: House of Anansi Press, 2003.

Kovach, Margaret. *Indigenous Methodologies: Characteristics, Conversations, and Contexts*. Toronto, ON: University of Toronto Press, 2010.

Krupat, Arnold. *For Those Who Come After: A Study of Native American Autobiography*. Berkeley, CA: University of California Press, 1985.

Krupat, Arnold, and Brian Swann, eds. *I Tell You Now: Autobiographical Essays by Native American Writers*. Lincoln, NE: University of Nebraska Press, 2005. First published 1987.

LaBoucane-Benson, Patti-Ann, N. Sherren, and D. Yerichuk. *Trauma, Child Development, Healing and Resilience: A Review of Literature with Focus on Indigenous Peoples and Communities*. Edmonton, AB: PolicyWise for Children & Families, 2017.

LaRocque, Emma. "Preface or Here Are Our Voices Who Will Hear?" In *Writing the Circle: Native Women of Western Canada, an Anthology*, edited by Jeanne Perreault and Sylvia Vance, xv–xxx. Edmonton, AB: NeWest Publications, 1990.

———. "Teaching Aboriginal Literature: The Discourse of Margins and Mainstreams." In *Creating Community: A Roundtable on Canadian Aboriginal Literature*, edited by Renate Eigenbrod and Jo-Ann Episkenew, 209–34. Penticton, BC: Theytus Books and Bearpaw, 2002.

Lawrence, Bonita. "Gender", Race, and the Regulation of Native Identity in Canada and the United States An Overview." *Hypatia* 18, no. 2 (2003): 3–31.

———. *"Real" Indians and Others: Mixed-Blood Urban Native Peoples and Indigenous Nationhood*. Vancouver, BC: University of British Columbia Press, 2004.

Lazorowich, Alexandra, dir. *Cree Code Talkers*. 2016; Winnipeg, MB: National Screen Institute Indigidocs. Film. http://nsifilms.ca/cree-code-talker/

Lutz, Hartmut. *Contemporary Challenges: Conversations with Canadian Native Authors*. Saskatoon, SK: Fifth House, 1991.

Macdougall, Brenda. *One of the Family: Metis Culture in Nineteenth-Century Northwestern Saskatchewan*. Vancouver, BC: University of British Columbia Press, 2010.

———. "Wahkootowin: Family and Cultural Identity in Northwestern Saskatchewan Metis Communities." *Canadian Historical Review* 87, no. 3 (2006): 431–62.

Mann, Charles C. *1491: New Revelations of the Americas before Columbus*. New York, NY: Knopf, 2005.

Maracle, Lee. *Bobbi Lee: Indian Rebel; Struggles of a Native Canadian Woman*. Recorded and edited by Don Barnett and Rick Sterling. Richmond, BC: LSM Information Center, 1975.

———. "Native Myths: Trickster Alive and Crowing." In *Language in Her Eye: Writing and Gender*, edited by Libby Scheier, Sarah Sheard, and Eleanor Wachtel, 182–87. Toronto, ON: Coach House, 1990.

———. "You Become the Trickster." In *Sojourner's Truth and Other Stories*, 11–13. Vancouver, BC: Press Gang, 1990.

McCall, Sophie. *First Person Plural: Aboriginal Storytelling and the Ethics of Collaborative Authorship*. Vancouver, BC: University of British Columbia Press, 2011.

McCall, Sophie, Deanna Reder, David Gaertner, and Gabrielle L'Hirondelle Hill, eds. *Read Listen Tell: Indigenous Stories from Turtle Island*. Waterloo, ON: Wilfrid Laurier University Press, 2017.

McHugh, Kathleen. "Profane Illuminations: History and Collaboration in James Luna and Isaac Artenstein's 'The History of the Luiseño People.'" *Biography* (2008): 429–460.

McKegney, Sam. *Magic Weapons: Aboriginal Writers Remaking Community after Residential School*. Winnipeg, MB: University of Manitoba Press, 2007.

McLeod, Neal. "Cree Narrative Memory." *Oral History Forum d'histoire orale* (2000): 37–61.

———. "Exploring Cree Narrative Memory." PhD diss., University of Regina, 2005.

———, ed. *Indigenous Poetics in Canada*. Waterloo, ON: Wilfrid Laurier University Press, 2014.

———. Introduction to *Indigenous Poetics in Canada*, edited by Neal McLeod, 1–14. Waterloo, ON: Wilfrid Laurier University Press, 2014.

Miller, David R. "Edward Ahenakew's Tutelage by Paul Wallace: Reluctant Scholarship, Inadvertent Preservation." *Gathering Places: Aboriginal and Fur Trade Histories* (2010): 249–72.

Minde, Emma. *Kwayask ê-kî-pê=kiskinowâpahtihicik—Their Example Showed Me the Way: a Cree Woman's Life Shaped by Two Cultures*. Edited and translated by Freda Ahenakew and H. C. Wolfart. Edmonton, AB: University of Alberta Press, 1997.

Moses, Daniel David, and Terry Goldie. *An Anthology of Canadian Native Literature in English*. 2nd ed. Toronto, ON: Oxford University Press, 1998.

Mosionier, Beatrice Culleton. *In Search of April Raintree: Critical Edition*. Edited by Cheryl Suzack. Winnipeg, MB: Portage and Main, 1999.

Mountain Horse, Mike. *My People, the Bloods*. Calgary, AB: Glenbow-Alberta Institute; Standoff, AB: Blood Tribal Council, 1979.

Nelson, George, Jennifer S. H. Brown, and Robert Brightman. *"The Orders of the Dreamed": George Nelson on Cree and Northern Ojibwa Religion and Myth, 1823*. St. Paul, MN: Minnesota Historical Society, 1988.

Nest, Michael, with Deanna Reder and Eric Bell. *Cold Case North: The Search for James Brady and Absolom Halkett*. Regina, SK: University of Regina Press, 2020.

Neuhaus, Mareike. "Reading the Prairies Relationally: Louise Bernice Half and 'Spacious Creation.'" *Canadian Literature* 215 (Winter 2012): 86–102, 203.

O'Brien, Lynne Woods. *Plains Indian Autobiographies*. Boise, ID: Boise State College, 1973.

Owl, Grey. *Tales of an Empty Cabin*. New York, NY: Dodd, Mead, 1936.

Papaschase First Nation. "Homepage." Accessed August 6, 2020. https://papas chase.ca

Petrone, Penny, ed. *First People, First Voices*. Toronto, ON: University of Toronto Press, 1983.

——. *Native Literature in Canada: From the Oral Tradition to the Present*. Toronto, ON: Oxford University Press, 1990.

Portillo, Annette Angela. *Sovereign Stories and Blood Memories: Native American Women's Autobiography*. Albuquerque, NM: University of New Mexico Press, 2017.

"Programme des activités." 3rd International Feminist Book Fair, June 14 to 19, 1988, Montreal. https://issuu.com/rimaathar/docs/programme _des_activites_3rdinternat

Quaife, Darlene Barry. *Bone Bird*. Winnipeg, MB: Turnstone, 1989.

Ratt, Solomon. "I'm Not an Indian." In *Read Listen Tell: Indigenous Stories from Turtle Island*, edited by McCall, Sophie, Deanna Reder, David Gaertner, and Gabrielle L'Hirondelle Hill. 170–72. Waterloo, ON: Wilfrid Laurier University Press, 2017. See also https://creeliteracy.org/2012/01/20/ another-story-from-solomon-ratt/

Razack, Sherene H. "Gendered Racial Violence and Spatialized Justice: The Murder of Pamela George." In *Race, Space and the Law: Unmapping a White Settler Society*, edited by Sherene H. Razack, 121–56. Toronto, ON: Between the Lines, 2002.

Reder, Deanna. "Indigenous Autobiography in Canada: Recovering Intellectual Traditions." In *The Oxford Handbook of Canadian Literature*, edited by Cynthia Sugars, 170–190. New York, NY: Oxford University Press, 2016.

——. "Native American Autobiography: Connecting Separate Critical Conversations." In *Lifewriting Annual: Biographical and Autobiographical Studies*, edited by Carol DeBoer-Langworthy and Thomas R. Smith, 35–63. Vol. 4. New York, NY: AMS Press, 2015.

——. "Understanding Cree Protocol in the Shifting Passages of 'Old Keyam.'" *Studies in Canadian Literature* 31, no. 1 (2006): 50–64.

———. "Writing Autobiographically: A Neglected Indigenous Intellectual Tradition." In *Across Cultures/Across Borders: Canadian Aboriginal and Native American Literatures*, edited by Paul DePasquale, Renate Eigenbrod, and Emma LaRocque, 153–70. Peterborough, ON: Broadview, 2010.

Reder, Deanna and Alix Shield. "'I write this for all of you': Recovering the Unpublished RCMP Incident in Maria Campbell's Halfbreed (1973)." *Canadian Literature* 237 (2019): 13–25. https://canlit.ca/article/i-write-this-for -all-of-you-recovering-the-unpublished-rcmp-incident-in-maria-camp bells-halfbreed-1973/

Sarris, Greg. *Keeping Slug Woman Alive: A Holistic Approach to American Indian Texts*. Berkeley, CA: University of California Press, 1993.

Saskatoon Daily Star. "Kindly, Yet Severe Criticism of Treatment of Indians is Voiced by Native Clergyman." 1 June 1918, 6.

Scheier, Libby, Sarah Sheard, and Eleanor Wachtel, eds. *Language in Her Eye: Writing and Gender*. Toronto, ON: Coach House, 1990.

Scofield, Gregory. *Thunder Through My Veins: Memories of a Métis Childhood*. Toronto, ON: HarperFlamingo Canada, 1999.

Settee, James. "Settee's Life (1891)." National Archives of Canada, MG 29 B15 Vol. 54 and relevant files.

Shield, Kathryn. "Kwaskastahsowin ('Put things to right'): Case Studies in Twentieth-Century Indigenous Women's Writing, Editing, and Publishing in Canada." PhD diss., Simon Fraser University, 2020.

Silman, Janet, ed. *Enough is Enough: Aboriginal Women Speak Out*. Toronto, ON: Women's Press, 1987.

Simpson, Leanne Betasamosake. "Indigenous Resurgence and Co-resistance." *Critical Ethnic Studies* 2, no. 2 (Fall 2016), 19–34.

Sing, Pamela V. "Intersections of Memory, Ancestral Language, and Imagination; or, the Textual Production of Michif Voices as Cultural Weaponry." *Studies in Canadian Literature* 31, no. 1 (2006): 95–115.

Stevenson (Wheeler), Winona L. "Calling Badger and the Symbols of the Spirit Language: The Cree Origins of the Syllabic System" *Oral History Forum d'histoire orale*. 2000. 19–24.

———. "The Church Missionary Society Red River Mission and the Emergence of a Native Ministry 1820-1860, with a case study of Charles Pratt of Touchwood Hills." MA thesis, University of British Columbia, 1988.

———. "Decolonizing Tribal Histories." PhD diss., University of California, Berkeley, 2000.

St. Peter, Christine. "Feminist Afterwords: Revisiting *Copper Woman*." In *Undisciplined Women: Tradition and Culture in Canada*, edited by Pauline Greenhill and Dianne Tye, 65–72. Montreal, QC & Kingston, ON: McGill-Queen's University Press, 1997.

———. "'Women's Truth' and the Native Tradition: Anne Cameron's *Daughters of Copper Woman*." *Feminist Studies* 15, no. 3 (1989): 499–523.

Swain, Molly Suzanne. "Victims of Deceit and Self-Deceit: The Role of the State in Undermining Jim Brady's Radical Métis Socialist Politics." MA thesis, University of Alberta, 2018.

Taylor, Drew Hayden. "Alive and Well: Native Theatre in Canada." *Journal of Canadian Studies* 31, no. 3 (1996): 29–37.

Teuton, Christopher B. *Deep Waters: The Textual Continuum in American Indian Literature.* Lincoln, NE: University of Nebraska Press, 2010.

Thornton, John P. "The National Policy, the Department of the Interior and Original Settlers: Land Claims of the Metis, Green Lake Saskatchewan, 1909-1930." MA Thesis, University of Saskatchewan, 1997.

Van Kirk, Sylvia. *Many Tender Ties: Women in Fur-trade Society, 1670–1870.* Norman, OK: University of Oklahoma Press, 1983.

Walker, Cheryl. *Indian Nation: Native American Literature and Nineteenth-Century Nationalisms.* Durham, NC: Duke University Press, 1997.

Warley, Linda. "Before Secret Path: Residential School Memoirs from the 1970s" In *On the Other Side(s) of 150: Untold Stories and Critical Approaches to History, Literature, and Identity in Canada,* edited by Linda M. Morra and Sarah Henzi, 285–99. Wilfrid Laurier University Press, 2021.

Warrior, Robert. *The People and the Word: Reading Native Nonfiction.* Minneapolis, MN: University of Minnesota Press, 2005.

——. *Tribal Secrets: Recovering American Indian Intellectual Traditions.* Minneapolis, MN: University of Minnesota Press, 1995.

Waubageshig, ed. *The Only Good Indian: Essays by Canadian Indians.* Toronto, ON: New Press, 1970.

Wawryshyn, L.A. "Eyes of Province Focus on School House: Teacher Charged with Giving Youth 104 Lashes." *The Springfield Leader.* 28 January 1947.

Wenger-Nabigon, Annie. "The Cree Medicine Wheel as an Organizing Paradigm of Theories of Human Development," *Native Social Work Journal* Vol. 7 (2010): 153–54.

Whitecalf, Sarah. *mitoni niya nêhiyaw-nêhiyaw-iskwêw mitoni niya/Cree is Who I Truly Am—Me, I am Truly a Cree Woman.* Edited by H.C. Wolfart and Freda Ahenakew. Winnipeg, MB: University of Manitoba Press, 2021.

Williams, Alex, dir. *The Pass System.* 2015; Peterborough, ON: Tamarack Productions. Film.

Wilson, Shawn. *Research is Ceremony: Indigenous Research Methods.* Halifax, NS: Fernwood, 2008.

Wolfart, H. C. "Cree Literature." In *Encyclopedia of Literature in Canada,* edited by W. H. New, 243–47. Toronto, ON: University of Toronto Press, 2002.

Womack, Craig. *Red on Red: Native American Literary Separatism.* Minneapolis, MN: University of Minnesota Press, 1999.

Wong, Hertha Dawn. *Sending my Heart Back Across the Years: Tradition and Innovation in Native American Autobiography.* New York, NY: Oxford University Press, 1992.

Young, James O., and Conrad G. Brunk, eds. *The Ethics of Cultural Appropriation.* New York, NY: Wiley-Blackwell, 2012.

Index

page numbers in *italics* indicate photos

Absolon, Kathleen, 31

Acco, Anne, 155n3

âcimisowina (autobiographical storytelling): as act of autonomy, 18; and author's mother's stories, 6–7; author's search for within Cree writing, 9, 10–11; author's use of her own life story to study Indigenous texts, 8–9; as favourite genre of Indigenous writers, 7, 11, 18; *Halfbreed* as most influential example of, 41, 52, 133; lessons embedded in, 7; as part of Indigenous intellectual tradition, 133; undervalued and understudied, 7–8, 18; use of to critique power structures, 8; written by E. Ahenakew, 61. *See also* Indigenous autobiography

âcimowina (factual stories), 6, 7

Ahenakew, Edward: autobiographical nature of *Black Hawk*, 85–86, 134; belief in respect between people, 73–75; distribution of his work after death, 79; earliest writing, 80–81; early years of, 61, 79; first two versions of his autobiography, 61; how his view of Indigenous health conditions was edited, 66–68; how his view of residential schools was edited, 68–71; how the unpublished manuscript *Old Keyam* relates to, 150n15; legacy, 79, 134; as mediator between Cree and colonizer, 74–76; resilience of, 60–61; respect for Indigenous mysticism, 75–76; response to D. C. Scott, 62–63; risks taken by in writing opinions, 64; R. M. Buck misrepresents how she edits, 71; R. M. Buck misrepresents the condition of his manuscript, 150n16; and sense of Cree spirituality, 93; stories about Napaskis, 84–85; trying to get published, 82; at U of A medical school, 81–82, 153n27; use of cross racial romance in novels, 83–84, 86, 134; writing in his 40s, 82; writing on Indigenous dances, 71–73. *See also Black Hawk* (Ahenakew); *Old Keyam* (Ahenakew)

Ahenakew, Freda, 11

alcohol, 33–34, 116

Anderson, Kim, 55

Angel, Michael, 30–31

âniskwâcimopicikêwin (intertextuality), 80, 91, 110, 134

Apess, William, 30, 145n34

Archibald, Jo-ann, 146n47

Archibald-Barber, Jesse Rae, 32

Armstrong, Jeannette, 124, 125, 126

âtayôhkêwina (sacred stories), 6, 11, 82

autobiography theory, 8, 128

Beck, Gwendoline, 109

Beeds, Tasha, 44, 75, 141n1

Bell, Bella, *114*, 129

Bell, Eric, 105–7

Bell, Gerry, 129

Bell, Gloria Jane, 35

Bell, Joanne, 129, *130*

Bell, Joe, 23, *24*

Bell, Kathy, *24*

Bell, Richard, *24*, 116

Bell, Robert, 35

Bidwell, Kristina Fagan, 32, 87, 154n33

Bill C-31, 42, 147n2, 147n3

Books in the Indigenous Studies Series

Blockades and Resistance: Studies in Actions of Peace and the Temagami Blockades of 1988–89 / Bruce W. Hodgins, Ute Lischke, and David T. McNab, editors / 2003 / xi + 276 pp. / illus. / ISBN 0-88920-381-4

Indian Country: Essays on Contemporary Native Culture / Gail Guthrie Valaskakis / 2005 / x + 293 pp. / illus. / ISBN 0-88920-479-9

Walking a Tightrope: Aboriginal People and Their Representations / Ute Lischke and David T. McNab, editors / 2005 / xix + 377 pp. / illus. / ISBN 978-0-88920-484-3

The Long Journey of a Forgotten People: Métis Identities and Family Histories / Ute Lischke and David T. McNab, editors / 2007 / viii + 386 pp. / illus. / ISBN 978-0-88920-523-9

Words of the Huron / John L. Steckley / 2007 / xvii + 259 pp. / ISBN 978-0-88920-516-1

Essential Song: Three Decades of Northern Cree Music / Lynn Whidden / 2007 / xvi + 176 pp. / illus., musical examples, links to audio tracks / ISBN 978-0-88920-459-1

From the Iron House: Imprisonment in First Nations Writing / Deena Rymhs / 2008 / ix + 147 pp. / ISBN 978-1-55458-021-7

Lines Drawn upon the Water: First Nations and the Great Lakes Borders and Borderlands / Karl S. Hele, editor / 2008 / xxiii + 351 pp. / illus. / ISBN 978-1-55458-004-0

Troubling Tricksters: Revisioning Critical Conversations / Linda M. Morra and Deanna Reder, editors / 2009 / xii+ 336 pp. / illus. / ISBN 978-1-55458-181-8

Aboriginal Peoples in Canadian Cities: Transformations and Continuities / Heather A. Howard and Craig Proulx, editors / 2011 / viii + 256 pp. / illus. / ISBN 978-1-055458-260-0

Bridging Two Peoples: Chief Peter E. Jones, 1843–1909 / Allan Sherwin / 2012 / xxiv + 246 pp. / illus. / ISBN 978-1-55458-633-2

The Nature of Empires and the Empires of Nature: Indigenous Peoples and the Great Lakes Environment / Karl S. Hele, editor / 2013 / xxii + 350 pp. / illus. / ISBN 978-1-55458-328-7

The Eighteenth-Century Wyandot: A Clan-Based Study / John L. Steckley / 2014 / x + 306 pp. / ISBN 978-1-55458-956-2

Indigenous Poetics in Canada / Neal McLeod, editor / 2014 / xii + 404 pp. / ISBN 978-1-55458-982-1

Literary Land Claims: The "Indian Land Question" from Pontiac's War to Attawapiskat / Margery Fee / 2015 / x + 318 pp. / illus. / ISBN 978-1-77112-119-4

Arts of Engagement: Taking Aesthetic Action In and Beyond Canada's Truth and Reconciliation Commission / Dylan Robinson and Keavy Martin, editors / 2016 / viii + 376 pp. / illus. / ISBN 978-1-77112-169-9

Learn, Teach, Challenge: Approaching Indigenous Literature / Deanna Reder and Linda M. Morra, editors / 2016 / xii + 580 pp. / ISBN 978-1-77112-185-9

Violence Against Indigenous Women: Literature, Activism, Resistance / Alison Hargreaves / 2017 / xv + 282 pp. / ISBN 978-1-77112-239-9

Read, Listen, Tell: Indigenous Stories from Turtle Island / Sophie McCall, Deanna Reder, David Gaertner, and Gabrielle L'Hirondlle Hill, editors / 2017 / xviii + 390 pp. / ISBN 978-1-77112-300-6

The Homing Place: Indigenous and Settler Literary Legacies of the Atlantic / Rachel Bryant / 2017 / xiv + 244 pp. / ISBN 978-1-77112-286-3

Why Indigenous Literatures Matter / Daniel Heath Justice / 2017 / xxii + 284 pp. / ISBN 978-1-77112-176-7

Activating the Heart: Storytelling, Knowledge Sharing, and Relationship / Julia Christensen, Christopher Cox, and Lisa Szabo-Jones, editors / 2018 / xvii + 210 pp. / ISBN 978-1-77112-219-1

Indianthusiasm: Indigenous Responses / Hartmut Lutz, Renae Watchman, and Florentine Strzelczyk, editors / 2020 / x + 252 pp. / ISBN 978-1-77112-399-0

Literatures, Communities, and Learning: Conversations with Indigenous Writers / Aubrey Jean Hanson / 2020 / viii + 182 pp. / ISBN 978-1-77112-449-2

I Am a Damn Savage/What Have You Done to My Country? / An Antane Kapesh; Sarah Henzi, translation and afterword / 2020 / vi + 314 pp. / ISBN 978-1-77112-408-9

Autobiography as Indigenous Intellectual Tradition: Cree and Métis âcimisowina / Deanna Reder / 2022 / xii + 182 pp. / ISBN 978-1-77112-554-3